IS SHE THE ONE?

Choosing a Wife without Wrecking Your Life

Toby Cavanaugh

IS SHE THE ONE?
by Toby Cavanaugh

Published by The International Localization Network
through Five Stones Publishing, www.ILNcenter.com

Printed in the United States of America

ISBN 9781935018346

Copyright © 2010 by Toby Cavanaugh
All rights reserved.

Unless otherwise indicated, Bible quotations are taken from
the *Holy Bible, New International Version* © 1973, 1978, 1984
by International Bible Society. Used by permission.
Also quoted is the *New American Standard Bible,*
© 1960, 1962, 1963, 1968, 1971, 1972, 1973, 1975, 1977, 1995
by The Lockman Foundation. Used by permission.

*To Micaela,
my treasure and
the definition of a great wife.
You are my #1 qualification
for writing this book.*

Contents

Preface. 7
Navigating Treacherous Waters 9
Test 1: Bible Test. 17
Test 2: Obedience Test 37
Test 3: Leaders Test 55
Test 4: Watchman Test 71
Test 5: Friends Test 79
Test 6: Carpool Test 87
Test 7: The List Test 97
Test 8: Fuzzy Math Test 111
Test 9: Romance Test 125
How to Use this Book 137

Preface

This book is for young men.

Most of my female Christian friends have amassed a small library of dating/marriage/if-I-can't-do-it-then-I'll-read-about-it books that they have devoured through their teen and college years. These books are not written for men. They have pictures of piggyback rides and walks on the beach and picnics and flowers and rings. Usually they are pastel colored with writing shaded somewhere between mauve and salmon. I mean, sure, I like to eat picnic food, vacation by the ocean, and imagine my wife draped on my back, but these books are obviously not for me.

This book aims to help young men choose a wife wisely. Girls, you are welcome to read it, too. I think many of the principles it contains are timeless wisdom for both genders. But don't think I am being sexist — the book just wasn't written for you!

This book is not about preparing yourself for marriage. Becoming a man of excellence is the key to actually having a chance at the kind of girl suggested in this book. If you don't pursue that, you won't even have the opportunity to choose.

This book is not about dating or courting. There are already books about that far better than I can write.

It is about choosing. There will come a day in your life when you get down on one knee, pull out the ring, and pop the question. I wrote this book so that you will never regret that day.

I wrote this book for young men who want to do something great with their lives, but, like me, have found it quite easy to make mistakes when it comes to their relationships with girls. I hope the lessons I have learned from studying Scripture, talking to men wiser than I am, and making more than my fair share of mistakes will save you from choosing a bride who limits your usefulness to God, success in life, and sense of fulfillment.

Instead, I pray this book does a small part in helping you find a wife who will double your usefulness, happiness, and success. I hope you enjoy it.

NAVIGATING TREACHEROUS WATERS

It was Good Friday. My two best friends, Matt and Ben, ran with me behind the garage to find it. There she was glistening in the early spring sun.

Our red canoe.

The three of us hoisted it on top of my family's minivan, and we took off for the river. On a whim, we had decided to grab Ben's canoe and paddle down a small local river that was overflowing with the rush of water from the spring thaw. The plan was to follow the river from a waterfall in one small town to a waterfall in another small town less than a ten-minute drive away. We parked the minivan at our destination, took Ben's car to the starting point, and set off on our adventure.

None of us was an experienced boater. We knew we were in over our heads as soon as our small red canoe took off out of control in the surging waters. If the surging waters and our total lack of experience were not enough to put fear in our hearts, the sight we saw as we rounded the river's first bend certainly did.

I saw it first. And I just pointed with my mouth gaping open. My friends followed my finger until their awed eyes showed they had caught the same sight. We shot down the river in stunned silence.

An exact replica of our red canoe dangled three feet out of the water, wrapped around a gnarled tree limb.

It looked like a tornado had picked it up and twisted it around the tree. We glanced at each other as our hearts quivered. But we had no time for fear because the river was sweeping us away.

And the adventure began.

We shot around bend after bend of the river, steering our small craft past the dozens of fallen trees that crisscrossed the river. We paddled and leaned and prayed to avoid obstacle after obstacle on a river ride that put roller coasters to shame.

Then we rounded a corner to find a fallen tree right in front of us. It bridged the whole river. We had no way to avoid it.

Matt and I both stuck our paddles in the water to slow us down. Ben quickly grabbed all our supplies. But in our effort to slow down, our canoe began to turn.

We smashed broadside into the tree and capsized.

I tumbled forward and was pinned underwater between the boat and tree. The power of the river had me trapped, and I needed air.

I began to panic. I kicked, wriggled and fought with all my strength. Finally, I jarred myself loose, and I popped up under the log to the other side. As I gasped my first breath, I saw that Matt and Ben had alertly swum down river and grabbed our paddles and supplies. Now they were waiting about one hundred feet downstream.

I needed to free the upside-down canoe so that we could meet downstream. But as hard as I pushed, it wouldn't budge. It was stuck.

My two friends waded back to the other side of the log to help me. We got ourselves poised to put all our strength into freeing the canoe.

One... Two... Three.... PUSH!

With a mighty heave, our capsized boat popped under the log. We dragged it to the riverbank on the other side of a log. There we quickly emptied out most of the water and continued on our journey.

This was the most exciting day I had experienced in years. I loved it. The adventure and excitement of flying through risky situations made me feel so alive.

We reached a slower part of the river. With the break in the action, we were having a blast reliving the fresh memories of the last hour.

But then the sun set. And the heat of the warm spring day quickly dissipated into a crisp, cold evening. We were soaking wet. We had been paddling for over two hours, our destination waterfall was nowhere in sight, and it was freezing cold.

I started out with a shivering feeling, but soon my entire body went numb. Each of us began to experience a new fear. Hypothermia on a small river only 10 minutes from our homes.

After another half-hour of paddling, our joints began to stiffen. The cold had sapped our strength, so we could no longer paddle. We set the paddles down in the boat, but our six hands were still gnarled as if gripping the paddles. Our fingers were so cold we could not straighten them.

For the first time in my life, I thought I might die. It was a ten-minute car ride, and it had already taken three hours by boat. Who knew how much longer it could be? I was bitterly cold and in pain. And I was afraid.

Thoughts began to swirl in my mind as my eyes peered ahead. "I might never make it home alive. I might never get married." All my regrets in life started coming to mind. If only I had...

But then I saw it.

The waterfall. We were saved.

We each grabbed a paddle and used our last reserves of strength to get the boat to the bank. Then we literally crawled up the hill to where the van was waiting. We changed our clothes, turned on the heat, and painfully began to thaw out. We had made it. Barely. And we now knew to respect the river.

Oftentimes, people approach relationships like I did the river. We jump in on a whim, get swept away with the excitement and adventure, and have no clue of the dangers that are lurking around the bend. And just like me, many find that the journey morphs into difficulty, pain, and fear.

This happens for two major reasons. We don't respect the danger of the river, and we don't know how to navigate the waters.

RESPECT THE DANGER

Many of us do not respect how serious a decision it is to choose a wife. When I was in college, I worked part-time as an assistant youth pastor for a church. Every day when I walked into work there was a framed poster hanging in the receptionist's area. It was a list called "The 21 Suggestions for Success."[1] And each day as I walked by, the number one suggestion would always catch my eye. Each time I read it, I would stop and think and make an oath to myself not to screw up that area. It said, "Marry the right person. This one

---

[1] H. Jackson Brown Jr.

decision will determine 90% of your happiness or misery." If 90% of my eggs are really in that one basket, then I want to make sure I get it right.

The Bible communicates the same thought. Proverbs 12:4 reads, "A wife of noble character is her husband's crown, but a disgraceful wife is like decay in his bones." The wife you choose will affect the quality of your life more than any other decision you make in life. A good wife will make you feel like a king, and a bad wife will make you feel like you are rotting from the inside out.

You can make your life a living hell by picking the wrong kind of wife. You can't even imagine the regret and pain that come from choosing poorly. Whether it is a life of fighting, bickering, and fading love or the devastating heartbreak and pain of a divorce, you will regret the day you said, "I do."

I remember an experience during the summer after my senior year of high school. I attended a concert of the Christian band Isaiah 6. Their lead singer and guitarist, Derek, was a family friend.

After the concert, I was standing in the parking lot with my friends when I saw the Isaiah 6 van pull up. Derek stuck his head out the window and called me over. He just wanted to talk.

We talked about the concert and basketball and my attempts to learn guitar. We talked about mutual friends and my plans for college.

Then Derek asked me, "So, do you have a girlfriend yet?"

I sheepishly let him know that I was still working on that. "Nah, man, I got nothing going in the girl department."

Then he said something that has stuck with me to this day.

"Be careful in your relationships with girls, Toby. They are the number one man-of-God killer."

I wanted to smile or crack a joke, but he said it so seriously, so earnestly, that I was afraid to break the silence that followed. I just nodded my head and soaked in his advice.

Relationships with girls are the number one man-of-God killer. Since that day, I have seen Derek's advice proven true countless times. Not only will your choices in women determine 90% of your happiness in life; it will also strongly affect your usefulness for God's kingdom.

I have seen my friends shipwreck their lives with wrong relationships. One got his girlfriend pregnant and had to drop out of college to marry her and take care of the baby. Another had his wife leave him for another guy less then a year after they were married. Another had to drop out of the ministry just to salvage his marriage to an emotionally wounded wife. Another is not even following the Lord anymore. A series of sinful relationships derailed his life.

With regret in their voices, I hear my friends tell me how difficult their marriages are. I watch them slowly sink into mediocre lives with their mediocre wives. As a friend, it is painful to see. I hear their horror stories and see their tears. Choosing poorly can bring tremendous pain and hardship. And it can sap the strength and energy that should be directed toward serving God.

This is not a book against marriage. Actually, I walked through my engagement and got married as I wrote this book. Marriage has the potential to be the most amazing, awesome blessing in your life. It is one of the greatest things that ever happened to me.

If you choose the right kind of woman for a wife, you can know fulfillment and happiness that few people get to experience. She can be an energizing force in your life. The intimacy, support, and fulfillment that she gives will carry over into every area. And experiencing the delights of a lover adds a dimension of special joy.

But I have also seen the other side: the pain, the frustration, the life detours, and the destruction. And it is not pretty.

I wrote this book not to scare you, but to protect you. The Scriptures contain wisdom that will help you choose a wife who will strengthen you, push you closer to God, and help you succeed in life.

NAVIGATING THE WATERS

Respecting the danger of the river is not enough. You also need to know how to navigate its waters. This book contains nine tests that will help you evaluate whether a girl is someone you should consider marrying. Each one rests on the insight of the Bible and time-tested wisdom.

Do you know that a lighthouse is only one part of helping to make a harbor safe? The lighthouse can never illuminate all the underwater reefs and rocks that can destroy a ship. What the boat needs is guidance along a safe path into a harbor. Only one approach angle is the safe route through the harbor; approach from other angles would be treacherous.

For centuries harbors have used a strategy to safely guide boats. They use other lights, called a "rear range." These lights stand on high poles in a straight line behind the lighthouse, and they enable the ship captain to know clearly the safe path through the harbor. How?

The captain merely needs to line up the lights. As long as he can see two or more lights, he knows that he is approaching at the wrong angle and will risk his ship if he proceeds. But when all the lights become one, he has found the safe passage and he can proceed with confidence.

Many harbors have only two lights. When the captain of the ship is still in the open sea, he maneuvers his ship until he can see only one light because the lights are aligned. Then he safely pulls into the harbor. But if the harbor has only two rear range lights, even when they appear to be aligned from a distance, he can be a hair off course. So if it were an especially dangerous harbor, it would have three or more lights. This would cause even the slightest deviation from the safe path to show up clearly.

The nine tests of this book will serve as harbor lights to guide you through the treacherous waters of finding the right type of girl to marry. If they all line up, then you have found your safe path. But if some of the tests are not lining up, be careful. Although the port of a great marriage is a wonderful place to live, the approaching harbor is filled with danger. Follow the safety of the harbor lights, and you can choose a girl with confidence.

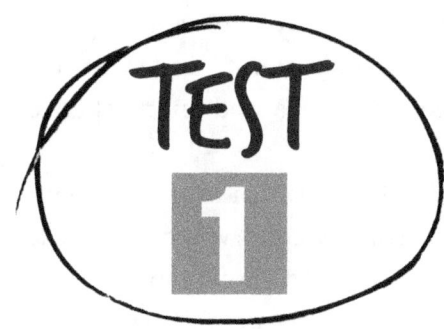

BIBLE TEST:
Is she the kind of girl Scripture would choose?

When I moved to Virginia Beach to attend graduate school, I bought a new desk at Mr. Second's. It was my first piece of furniture, and I liked it. The right side of the desk slides out four feet and creates an extra writing surface. It is a great idea, especially for a student who is unorganized and needs a place to put all his papers.

Anyway, my dad and I cut open this box and the first thing I saw was... Well, let me first say that my dad and I are not exactly handymen. We go by the philosophy of "Why fix something yourself, when you can pay someone else to do it." He is not nearly as bad as I am, but we are definitely not carpenters; we don't change our own oil; you get the idea. So we cut open this box, and the first thing I saw was Step 137 on the back of the instruction manual. That was not a typo — Step 137. It was an omen, but I still had no idea of what I was getting into. It was an 8-hour day later of sitting and fitting, screwing and gluing, tools and fools, staring and swearing, when I finally attached the last piece and collapsed on my stained carpet floor.

I knew two things at the end of that day that I did not know at the beginning. First, I will never do that again. Second, when it comes to a complex project, it is crucial to have an instruction manual.

God has given us in the Bible His instruction manual for choosing a great woman. Throughout the pages of His Word, God has inserted the wisdom we need to pick a wife we won't regret choosing. Not everyone knows this because these instructions are mixed in with so many other teachings. But if you will study and apply what it teaches, you will have taken a huge first step to picking a wife who won't ruin your life. And, luckily, there are fewer than 137 steps.

COMMANDS OF SCRIPTURE

As I studied the Scriptures about marriage, relationships, and finding a spouse, there was only one true command that the Bible gives to young people in picking a life partner. God's word communicates only one thing to us as an absolutely necessary, no-compromise, you-are-in-disobedience-if-you-don't-do-this characteristic of your wife to be.[2] If you are a Christian, then she must be, too.

Several places in Scripture communicate this, but one says it clear as Windexed glass. The Apostle Paul writes in 1 Corinthians

---

[2] The Bible also says that you should not marry a woman who has been married and divorced for reasons other than "marital unfaithfulness" (Matthew 5:32; 19:9) or abandonment (1 Corinthians 7:15). But this is not a normal situation for young men, so I chose not to address it here.

7:39, "A woman is bound to her husband as long as he lives. But if her husband dies, she is free to marry anyone she wishes, but he must belong to the Lord." This passage is actually talking about widowed women. It says after their husbands died, they can marry anyone that they want, but "he must belong to the Lord." Or he must be a Christian.

You probably wonder, "What does the rule for a widowed woman have to do with me?" Well, to fully understand the gravity of this statement, you need to know a little bit about the culture in that day. Because of serious discrimination against women, it was virtually impossible for a woman to have an adequate job. Her husband or family was her only source of support. When a woman lost her husband, she lost the source of all her income.

The situation was not like today, where she might receive a large insurance payment or government assistance. She could not simply go out and get a job to support herself. She would have to quickly marry again or turn to family members to meet all her needs. If those two options were unavailable, she would be forced into horrible jobs, begging, or even prostitution just to survive in poverty.

The author Paul says to people in such a situation, even they must marry Christians. He is saying that no matter how extreme your circumstances are, how desperately you need to be married, or how lonely you feel, your spouse *must* be a Christian. No exceptions. If no exception exists for the widow who might be banished to utter poverty, it definitely is not there for young men like you and me.

Why is Paul so extreme about this? Because he understood the spiritual law of gravity. It is always easier to be pulled down than pulled up. If I stand on a chair and link hands with a friend standing on the ground, it takes much less effort for my friend to pull me off the chair than for me to pull him up. Why? Because he has gravity working with him. The same is true spiritually. You may think that as a believer you will pull your unsaved girlfriend up to your level, but the reality is you will much more often be pulled down to her level. Gravity is working against you.

As I was writing this chapter, I found out that my friend, who is a new Christian, started dating an unbeliever while I was away on a one-month trip. So several nights ago he came to my apartment, we sat down together, and I shared with him the passages I just wrote about.

You could literally see the look of pain come over his face. He clearly understood what God said in His Word, but he just as clearly wanted to be with this girl.

He said, "Toby, it's not easy for someone like me to find a girlfriend. I can't give her up. God needs to make her become a Christian!"

"We will pray for her to know Jesus too, but the important thing is that you obey Jesus now. If you don't, you will suffer," I responded.

He shook his head as if that would make the choice any easier and said, "I know that she will not drag me down. I promise that I can stand." After another hour of talking more about the situation, he left for home to pray about it.

I did not see him again until yesterday when we wept together over the pain he had suffered in the last 72 hours. After he left my house that night, he went home and asked God to show him what to do (as if the Bible were not already clear enough). He opened his Bible at random to a verse in Proverbs commanding him to flee from the woman who would destroy him. God was making this extra clear for him.

But the next night he went out with her. They ended up going back to his dorm room and sleeping together.

As he sat next to me on the bed, he told me he knew what he had done was wrong. He did not stand. He was dragged down. Despite all his promises, it took less than 24 hours. After finding out more about the kind of girl she is, he is fearfully awaiting the results of an HIV test.

Do not think you are the exception. Do not think you are the one who can stand firm when everyone else has failed. You are taking a one-way path to destruction. Please do not make the same mistake as my friend.

Not only will an unsaved girlfriend or wife have a negative influence on you spiritually, but as a couple, you will have a major disconnect in the most significant area of your life. Your core beliefs that govern how you will use your time, spend your money, raise your children, and make decisions in life are like two discordant notes on a piano. You will be constantly at odds.

If you choose to date or marry a non-Christian girl, you are directly disobeying the Word of God. You will be dragged down into an anemic faith or doomed to disconnection from your wife in everything important. Trust me (or ask anyone who has made that choice). It will not work out well.

ADVICE OF SCRIPTURE

While the Bible does not give many commands for choosing a wife, it offers plenty of wisdom and advice. As I studied the Bible, and especially the wisdom of Proverbs, I found three characteristics that the Bible highlights in recognizing a godly woman. Scripture mentions a few other qualities of a great wife, but these three are listed repeatedly in God's Word.

1. Purity

The book of Proverbs dedicates more space to talking about the dangers of an impure girl than any other topic. All of chapters 5 and 7 and half of chapter 6 are totally dedicated to this theme. They warn of the woman who tries to sexually entice a young man.

Although it gives different examples, the message is always that allowing yourself to be seduced by this impure woman will destroy you. The Bible says that she is like a deep pit, a path to the grave, bitter gall, a double-edged sword, hot coals, and a highway to hell. And those are just a sampling of the metaphors. The author of Proverbs tries to say in every way possible, "Don't go near her! She will destroy you!"

In describing this type of woman, the Proverbs give us some clues for recognizing her. First, it says that she has a "smooth tongue."[3] In another passage it says, "[Her] lips drip honey, and her speech is smoother than oil."[4] This woman is impure in her speech. She knows how to entice a man with her words. She will say things to stir up a man's sexual desires. Then she can get his attention or whatever else she wants from him. She knows what to say to turn a guy on.

Second, it says, "Do not lust in your heart after her beauty."[5] This type of girl is often hot and knows how to use it. She takes her beautiful form, meant to bless her husband, and uses it to seduce men. This does not mean that we should suspect any beautiful woman of being impure. The thing that characterizes this woman is the way she uses her beauty. She knows how to use her body to stir up the lust in a man's heart.

---

[3] Proverbs 6:24
[4] Proverbs 5:3
[5] Proverbs 6:25a

Third, "Do not let her capture you with her eyelids."[6] You may wonder, "Eyelids? How does she capture me with her eyelids? If I can resist any part of her body, I can at least withstand eyelids." But this is referring to the flirty or insinuative way a girl can use her eyes. Perhaps the author has in mind seductively winking eyes or batting eyelashes. He might be referring to the ancient custom of painting the eyelids with makeup to make the eyes appear brilliant and alluring. Whatever his exact reference, his meaning is clearly the flirtatious and seductive use of the eyes. This woman knows how to flirt with a man to arouse his interest. Again, the Bible is not saying it is wrong to be friendly or wear makeup. The issue is the impure woman uses everything at her disposal to stir up the sexual longings of a man.

Fourth, it says she is "dressed like a prostitute."[7] The Hebrew word translated prostitute means a "sexually immoral female," not necessarily someone who is paid for sex. The impure woman is dressed like she wants sex. I think I don't need to put specifics to that. We all know what it is to see a girl who is dressed for sex. It can be tight, short, low, or missing. She is showing off what the Good Lord gave her. The problem is He gave it to her to share with her husband, not every guy with at least one eye who walks within 50 feet. Again, we see this woman using everything she has to arouse a guy's sexual interest.

Finally, this woman obviously is willing to give herself sexually to men. Perhaps she seduces men for the sex itself. It is more likely she uses sex to get what she wants from them. It could be a desperate attempt to build up a low self-image or a destructive search for true love. Maybe she will use sex to try to secure a husband for herself or to advance her career. It does not matter if her motives are evil, sad,

---

[6] Proverbs 6:25b - NASB
[7] Proverbs 7:10

or pitiful. She will destroy you! And you need to keep as far away from her as possible.

Why is this woman so dangerous? She destroys your character, seducing you to leave your own purity for a night of pleasure. She manipulates you. Her defining characteristic is that she uses sex to control. She will use that power to lead you into other sin and foolish decisions. She sidetracks you. With her sexual wiles, she steals your focus from positive things by dragging you into a negative relationship. She entraps you. You end up stuck in a relationship with a woman you don't respect.

Instead, pursue women who are characterized by their purity. The three major lists in the New Testament that describe how godly women behave all list modesty and purity as one of the primary characteristics.[8] The Bible advises us to choose a woman who values her purity more than attention from guys, more than feeling good about herself, and more than getting married. She should value it more than anything.

In the forests of northern Europe and Asia lives an animal called the ermine, known for her snow-white fur in winter. Because it is her protective camouflage, she instinctively protects her white coat against anything that would soil it. Fur hunters take advantage of this unusual trait of the ermine. They don't set a snare to catch her, but instead they find her home, which is usually a cleft in a rock or a hollow in an old tree. They smear the entrance and interior with grime. Then the hunters set their dogs loose to find and chase the ermine. The frightened animal flees toward home but doesn't enter because of the filth. Rather than soil her white coat, she is trapped by the dogs and captured while preserving her purity. For the ermine, her purity is even more precious than her life. Find a woman who

---

[8] 1 Timothy 2:9-15 & Titus 2:3-5 & 1 Peter 3:1-6

values her purity like the ermine, and you are setting yourself up for a life of faithfulness, closeness, and intimacy.

How can I tell if a girl is pure?

Ask yourself the following questions:

1. How does she dress?

2. What is her reputation?

3. What is her sexual history?
(not a question for the first date)

4. Does she use her body to get attention?

5. Does she give you the feeling of being easy?

6. Does she let you touch her in ways you should not?
(If you don't already know, then don't find out!)

7. Do her words insinuate sexual things?

---

2. Not Quarrelsome

Proverbs emphasizes the horrors of being married to a quarrelsome wife so much that it sounds like a broken record. Three separate proverbs warn against marrying this kind of woman and two of those are even repeated twice. Someone must have thought this was important.

If it is so important to avoid a wife like this, then you are going to want to know exactly what "quarrelsome" means. It is not a word we often use to describe someone today. The Hebrew word here has been translated by biblical experts as contentious, brawling, nagging, crabby, cranky, complaining, argumentative, bickering, and full of strife. Do you get the idea? Each of these biblical proverbs uses a word picture to teach us about the horrors of a quarrelsome wife.

The first says that "a quarrelsome wife is like a constant dripping on a rainy day" (27:15; see also 19:13). This proverb was written about 3,000 years ago when the materials and technology of construction were still quite primitive. Thus, it would be a relatively common thing to have a roof that leaked in steady rain. The proverb compares her to the annoying constancy of a repetitive drip. She nags and brings up the same negative thing repeatedly.

Drip… drip… drip…

She never stops her complaining, fighting and nagging. The next verse goes on to say, "Restraining her is like restraining the wind or grasping oil with the hand." Her negativity cannot be stopped. You might as well try to stop the wind or squeeze oil in your hand. It is impossible. The quarrelsome wife is both constantly negative and virtually impossible to change.

The second proverb says that it is "better to live on a corner of a roof than share a house with a quarrelsome wife" (21:9; 25:24). This highlights the misery to which you are sentencing yourself if you marry this kind of woman. Your home, like your wife, becomes a thing to escape rather than enjoy. The poor husband would rather live up on the roof of his house withstanding the worst of all the weather than have to live with his negative, bickering wife.

A few verses later, the third proverb takes the second one a step further. It reads, "Better to live in a desert than with a quarrelsome and ill-tempered wife" (21:19). Even the corner of his roof is not far enough removed from his miserable wife. It is better to be wasting away in the wilderness than to have to live with this kind of woman.

The desert is a place of oppressive and draining heat. But that is nothing compared to the oppressive nagging and draining negativity that is inflicted upon him by his life partner.

I can remember sitting in a restaurant across the table from a beautiful young woman. She was a believer, serving in ministry, and looked great. As I looked back at her face across the table, I could only think about one thing…

"How can I kill myself to escape this conversation?"

She was the most negative person I had ever met in my life. She complained about everything. The restaurant was too hot, then too cold. The water tasted weird. Her food wasn't cooked right. And this was just the first 5 minutes. Being with her somehow drained my very will to live. And this was one meal. When I imagine being married to someone like that… No! I don't want to imagine it. It would be worse than torture.

The wise author of Proverbs is trying to tell you something here. "Do not doom yourself to this fate. Refuse to marry a quarrelsome woman."

You may be thinking, "No one would ever marry a woman like that."

But we do. Look around you. All kinds of men are married to women like this. Maybe it was because she was hot. Or maybe he fell in love and ignored the obvious signs. Perhaps he thought she would change after they got married, or he underestimated her problem. Whatever the reason, it happened. He chose her. And even if he doesn't end up in the desert, he will still live to regret it.

> **How can I tell if a girl is quarrelsome?**
>
> **Ask yourself the following questions:**
>
> 1. Does she complain often?
>
> 2. Does she constantly correct you?
>
> 3. Do you ever feel nagged?
>
> 4. Is she easily made angry?
>
> 5. Do you feel like she often starts fights with you?
>
> 6. Does she regularly seem to have disputes with others?

3. Submissive

This book is not about gender equality or the roles of men and women in a Christian marriage. I am not trying to cause any problems or disagreements. But the fact is one of the three character traits most emphasized in the Bible for a godly wife is being submissive to her husband.

Actually, it is by far *the* most emphasized character quality for a godly wife in the New Testament. If it is so important, what does submission mean? Is it being a doormat? Is it only talking when spoken to? Is it something that is a couple millennia out of date?

The idea of wives submitting is found in at least seven places in the New Testament.[9] And in each place it is either explicitly stated or implied that the woman is to be submissive *to her husband*. This is not a stance she takes toward every man in life as though she is an inferior person. It is a specific relational role with her husband.

[9] 1 Cor. 11:2-16; 14:33-35; Eph. 5:22-24; Col. 3:18; 1 Tim. 2:9-15; Titus 2:4-5; & 1 Pet. 3:1-6

I believe 1 Peter explains the idea of submission most fully. The author discusses four different human relationships that should demonstrate submission. First, in 2:13-17 it teaches everyone to show submission to the government over them. Second, in 2:18-21 it tells slaves to be in submission to their masters. Third, in 3:1-6 it exhorts women to be submissive to their husbands. And fourth, in 5:5 young people to be submissive to their church leaders.

Inside these passages, we can find the keys to what submission is truly supposed to be.

First, these are not relationships of superiority. Just as my governing officials are not superior to me and neither are my pastors, a husband is in no way superior to his wife.

Second, these are relationships of respect and deference. This may chafe against some of today's prevalent beliefs, but the Bible does clearly teach that the wife should respect her husband in the same way that we should respect our elders and governing officials. For the marriage relationship to function properly, God saw it best to have the leadership and responsibility rest on the man.

It is like a dance. For a couple to be able to dance smoothly, the man has the responsibility of leading the dance. This allows the woman to know where she is going and gives her the freedom to dance with beauty.

But if the woman decides that she does not want to follow her partner's lead, what happens? Chaos. There will be crushed toes and maybe even a fall. The couple falls out of time with each other, and the beauty of the dance vanishes. They no longer move in harmony.

The Bible teaches that marriage is a dance that God designed for the man to lead. That does not make the man superior or even a better dancer. It is only a role he plays to give both partners the freedom to dance their part together.

Third, in each of the examples (government leaders, masters, husbands, and church leaders) a person is to submit out of reverence for God, not on the merits of the leader himself or herself. Basically, they should submit to them because God tells us to, not because the person necessarily deserves it. This idea permeates these passages in 1 Peter. It says we are to submit ourselves "for the Lord's sake," because we are "conscious of God," and because we "hope in God."

Fourth, God will greatly reward those who submit in difficult circumstances. It tells us that submission is "commendable before God," "being a servant of God," and "of great worth in God's sight." If a submissive person is taken advantage of in any relationship — parental, marriage, employment, government — then God will care for that person and give him or her great rewards in heaven.

Thus, submission is primarily an issue of trusting God. Does she trust God to care for her if she submits in a difficult situation? If not, she will act out of fear and grasp for the lead in the relationship. But if she trusts God, she can follow an imperfect leader knowing God will care for her.

One of the girls I dated had a difficult time trusting God enough to allow me to lead the relationship. Although she was not outwardly domineering, she would constantly grasp at control in the relationship. She wanted it to move faster than I felt God did, so she would subtly resist the direction I felt from the Lord through subversive ways. She would keep bringing up the subject after I told her what I felt the Lord was saying. She would often use outwardly gentle questions to try to attack my stance on the issue. She would even initiate physical contact in a way that would cause the relationship to progress to the next level. She was unwilling to let me lead our relationship because she was unwilling to trust the Lord to care for her and lead through me. She wanted control.

Fifth, the proper atmosphere for a wife's submission is when her husband overflows with consideration, selflessness, and unconditional love. All three of the passages in Scripture that directly exhort wives to submit to their husbands are followed by an exhortation to husbands as well.[10] They are commanded to "love your wives just as Christ loved the church," to "not be embittered against them," and to "be considerate toward your wives and treat them with respect." It makes it infinitely easier for a woman to trust God and submit when she knows she can trust her husband, too. How can you tell when a girl lacks a submissive attitude? When a woman is unsubmissive, it will often manifest itself in one of two ways depending on her personality. If she has an aggressive personality, it will show itself in active resistance. If she is more passive, then she will resist through manipulation like the girl I mentioned above. Either way, she is trying to seize control because she is unwilling to trust.

Like the woman who won't follow her dance partner's lead, an unsubmissive wife throws a beautiful act into chaos. But instead of stomped toes, the consequences are a strained marriage, an unhappy home, and unfulfillment in both partners.

I know one Christian family where the wife has been filled with unsubmissiveness for years. Her husband has slowly retreated to a quiet shell of what he could be. None of the children get along with the mother. Constant frustration and tension permeate the home. And she has slowly even destroyed herself as her rebellious attitude has polluted her own spiritual walk. An unsubmissive spirit will poison a marriage and family. Do not marry a woman who carries this venom.

Because a girl does not owe you submission as an acquaintance, friend, or even boyfriend, how can you tell if she will be a submissive

---

[10] Eph. 5:25-33; Col.; & 1 Pet. 3:7

wife? It is easy. Because submission is about obeying God and not about husbands, you can look at how she interacts with any authority. Does she submit to her parents, her boss, her government, her pastor and her elders? If not, she has an unsubmissive spirit.

How can I tell if a girl has a submissive spirit?

Ask yourself the following questions:

1. Does she disrespect or disobey her parents, especially her father?

2. Does she consistently have problems with her bosses at work, or do they get along well?

3. Does she tend to complain to you about the authority figures in her life? If she does, does she tend to obey them anyway, or does she rebel?

4. Would she be considered a "rebellious person"?

5. Does she have any adults besides her parents that she seeks out for advice and input as a leader?

Other Important Qualities

Even though purity, submission, and not being quarrelsome are by far the most emphasized virtues of a good wife in Scripture, other important insights rest in its pages. I want to touch on three other qualities of a godly woman that are taught in Scripture.

First, **a focus on inward beauty.** First Peter 3:3-4 says, "Your beauty should not come from outward adornment, such as braided hair and the wearing of gold jewelry and fine clothes. Instead, it should be that of your inner self, the unfading beauty of a gentle and quiet spirit, which is of great worth in God's sight." Peter is teaching women that they should focus on improving the beauty of their spirit rather than on their outward beauty. And guys can be taking notes on what kind of woman to be looking for, too.[11]

Does this mean that women should not wear jewelry, nice clothes or an attractive hairstyle? No. Peter is not forbidding these things. He is asking the question, "What is the source of your beauty?" Is it your clothes and hair? Or a gentle, Christ-like spirit? He lets us know what is better in God's sight. If we are planning to share the rest of our lives with someone, we should be looking for the right kind of beauty, too. I am not trying to play down the importance of being attracted to your girl. She should be intensely desirable to you. But what is the source of her beauty? Does she invest all her time in her outward appearance or growing more beautiful spiritually? All outward beauty fades away. Clothes get old, hair gets thin, and jewelry loses its luster. The dimples become wrinkles, and the curves become lumps. But inner beauty is "unfading." It only gets better and better as the years go by.

Second, they should have **control over their tongues,** especially in gossiping and slandering others. Three times in the New Testament, gossiping and slandering is specifically referred to in respect to women.[12] The Apostle Paul seems to think that gossip is a vice into which it is specifically easy for women to fall. This does not mean that all women have a problem with gossip or that only

---

[11] Also see 1 Timothy 2:9-10
[12] 1 Timothy 3:11; 5:13 & Titus 2:3

women struggle with this sin. But it does seem to indicate that, generally speaking, it is a bigger problem for women.

Almost every time that Paul talks about issues with women in the church, he mentions this issue of gossip and slander. First Timothy 3:11 gives a list of virtues to be found in female leaders and the wives of male leaders in the church. Of all the virtues he could list, he only gives four. And "not malicious talkers" is one of them. The Greek word translated "malicious talker" is only translated this way three times in the Bible, but it is translated as another word 35 times in the Bible.

The Devil.

That's right—the Devil. This Greek word means "the Devil." Paul is saying that women should not be little "devils," tearing down people with their words wherever they go. Who wants a wife that is a mini-devil? Paul forbids men with wives like that from being leaders in the church. Why? Because he knows she will bring shame to the husband and the church. If a girl has a tendency to violate trusts, use private information against people, and tear down others, do you really want to be her best friend? You will either spend your life hearing negative things about other people or having yourself torn down to others. And probably both. Sounds great, huh?

Third, they should be **industrious.** When I look at the description of the virtuous woman in Proverbs 31:10-31, her work ethic is the thing that stands out to me the most. She gets up before dawn and works until after dark. She makes food for the family, sews clothes for them, runs her own business, decorates her house, and takes care of the poor in her spare time. She is superwoman!

I do not think every guy should demand his wife be the Proverbs 31 ideal because then marriage would cease and the human race would be eradicated. In the same way, girls can't expect us to be the perfect reflection of Christ. No one can live up to an ideal. But we can expect that a girl be characterized by hard work rather than laziness.[13]

This does not need to be working around the house. The Bible does not teach that women should be forced to stay at home their entire married lives. That was the culture in which the Bible was written. The issue is not whether she is working at home or at a job. The question is, "Is she a good worker or is she lazy?"

When I was in college, I was taking one class online as a distance student due to a schedule conflict, even though I lived locally. Each class member was assigned a partner for a large class project. My partner was another distance student who lived about an hour away. We were supposed to meet online and over email to discuss our project. However, she would never show up online. I would email her and receive no replies. And I didn't know her phone number. I got more and more apprehensive as the due date for the project approached.

Finally, I could wait no longer. There was no time left. I had to do the whole project myself. So I killed myself for those last few days before the deadline to finish the project. Finally, I had to turn in the paper for both of us as if we were truly partners. I hate group projects.

When you marry a girl, you are getting a partner and team member. Before you commit to a lazy person, you need to decide, "Do I want to have to carry the weight for two people my whole life?" Marry a woman who will work hard to play her part on the team.

The Bible Test is all about adjusting our perspective to what the Bible teaches is important. Purity is worth more than chemistry. Hard work is more desirable than a hard body. Makeup washes off, but inner beauty is forever. Kind lips taste better than full ones. A

---

[13] See also 1 Timothy 5:13 & Titus 2:5

submissive spirit is to be treasured, and a quarrelsome woman is to be avoided at all costs.

If you ignore the instruction book, don't be surprised if the relationship ends up functioning poorly. But if you prioritize what the Bible says is important, you are much more likely to experience marriage as God intended it.

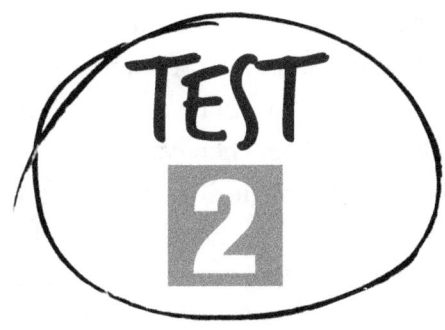

OBEDIENCE TEST:
Has God spoken directly to you?

There she was. My heart started beating faster and faster, pounding in my chest. She was just as beautiful as I remembered her. And she was all alone.

Her name was Jenna. She was a law school student who had class in the same building as I did. And she was perfect.

Two weeks prior, a mutual friend had introduced us in the atrium of our classroom building. She was everything I had ever wanted in a girl. She was a committed Christian. She was a brilliant student. She was an accomplished athlete. And it showed. She was so beautiful I found myself holding my breath every time I saw her. She even had a Southern accent.

Ever since that first encounter, I had been rushing out of every class pathetically hoping to see her again. Sometimes I would see her across the atrium talking with her friends. Her long, black, curly hair would wave back and forth as she talked. She always had a crowd of good-looking guys around her. I would just lean against the wall, sigh the deep sigh of infatuation, and look on longingly.

Over the two weeks my infatuation grew until I was no longer content to watch from afar. I had to talk to her. Then came the day where I walked into the atrium after class to find it empty. As I turned to disappointedly head back to my apartment, I suddenly gasped. Jenna walked into the atrium from around a corner. This was it.

Her…

Me…

Alone.

The Lord had answered my prayers. I took a step toward her, and a wave of fear swept over me.

"What am I doing?" I thought. "I can't talk to her. She won't even remember me." Then she looked at me.

She smiled. Out of instinct, I waved.

She waved back. And she started walking toward me.

"Oh no, now what do I do?" My mind raced as I thought of what to say. Like a computer rebooting, my brain emptied itself of every rational thought. I had nothing. And she was getting closer.

As she approached me, my entire body froze. I could no longer move my limbs. My heart was beating against my rib cage like a sledgehammer. I wanted to talk or walk or wave or something, but I was paralyzed in place.

She broke the silence with her soothing Southern tones, "Hey, Toooby. How ya been doing?"

By some miracle of God I was able to weakly squeak out, "Hi, Jenna. I'm good." A few awkward moments passed until I was able to add, "Uh, how about you?"

"Great, great, "she said, "I am about to go help some young girls at cheerleading camp. You knew I was a cheerleader in college, right?"

My mind was recovering by this point. I was able to interject, "No, I didn't, but you sure look like you could have been."

A smile more glorious than the sun lit up her face. She said, "Well, thanks, Toby. That makes a girl feel really good." Bam! Score one for Toby.

Then I remembered. It was Friday. I was feeling bold now. I said, "So… what are you doing this evening? Would you like to go out with me and some of my friends?" I began to plead with the Lord, "I will never ask anything again. Please let her say nothing. Please, please, please."

"Actually, Tobster, every Friday night I go and volunteer at a soup kitchen in the city with a couple girl friends. But I would love to hang out sometime."

"This girl is too good to be true," I thought to myself. "Wait! Did she just say she would love to hang out sometime? And did she just call me Tobster?"

Then like a fool, I didn't close the deal.

I simply said, "Ok, maybe some other time."

She looked disappointed and said, "OK… Well, I have to get running to cheerleading camp. Um, see ya."

"See ya," I said. She turned and began to walk away. No, this was wrong. I couldn't let this slip away. I blurted, "Wait!" She turned around. I stuttered, "Um, d… d… do you think I could have your ph…phone number?" Her face lit up.

"I would really like you to have that, Toby Cavanaugh." She grabbed a pen from her bag and ripped a small piece of paper from a little notebook. As she began to write, I walked over to where she was standing. She folded the paper in half and handed it to me, saying, "There you go, Bubba." Then she reached out her delicate hand and touched my left shoulder.

My whole body quivered. Then she ran her fingers down my arm to my elbow. My heart was going to beat out of my chest. She gave my elbow a little squeeze and turned to go. As she spun around, she flipped her hair, releasing a scent that took me to another world.

I came to my senses just in time to wave goodbye as she walked out the door. Then I felt a tingly, burning sensation in my left hand. I looked down. The number. I quickly unfolded it to read in fun, feminine handwriting, "Jenna Stevens - 555-2395." I sighed. Then I read it again. Then I ran my finger over the writing as if somehow touching her name made me closer to her.

I was in love.

Several days later, I was home in my apartment relaxing in my room. As I was sitting there, my thoughts turned (as they often did) to my new flame, Jenna. I began to think about calling her to see if she would want to go out. I had almost convinced myself that she would say, "Yes."

Then all of a sudden, I felt God speak to me. It was not an audible voice or a teleprompter in my mind. But immediately inside I knew without any doubt that He was telling me I should not pursue this relationship. Something rose up inside my heart that I had rarely experienced before. Rebellion.

"What do you mean I can't pursue this relationship?" I asked. "She is perfect. And I like her a ton."

Again, I felt God say, "Do not pursue this relationship."

I began to plead, "But, God, please. I won't do anything wrong. She is a Christian. She loves You. She is involved at her church. She even volunteers at the soup kitchen. There is no way this can be against Your will."

Again, He said, "Toby, do not pursue this relationship."

For the next half-hour there was a battle inside me like I had never experienced before. Part of me wanted so bad to be with Jenna. But the other part of me knew I must obey God at any cost. This wrestling match was so intense I thought my soul would be torn in two. I knew what I must do, but I could not bring myself to give up this other love. Finally, I submitted. I cried, "God, You know I will obey You no matter what. Even when You take the thing I want the most. I won't pursue this relationship." I felt like a part of me died that night.

However, over the next year I was able to observe the life of this young woman. I saw that in many ways she was not at all what she had seemed. By the end of that year, I praised God that He had directed my path away from someone who was not at all the type of person I wanted to marry. God had protected me by speaking directly into my life.

Marriage is the most significant life decision you will ever make, after choosing to follow Jesus Christ. It determines your future more than any other choice. And God is aware of this. He will go out of His way to protect you from making a life-destroying blunder in this area. Sometimes that will include Him communicating with you directly. Direct communication is God speaking to us without using another person. There is no middleman; it is straight from Him to you.

I want to say right up front that it is crucial that we test any direct communication from God against the clear teachings of the Bible. We must always test what we feel subjectively against what the Bible says objectively. God will never tell us to do anything that contradicts His Word. Scripture is the most clear and obvious communication we have from God. But sometimes the Holy Spirit chooses to speak to us in a personal way that will apply the teachings of the Bible to our lives.

God has spoken directly throughout history and today in several different ways.

1. Audible Voice

Examples abound all throughout Scripture where God speaks to people audibly. One biblical example is the story of Samuel as a young boy (1 Samuel 3). He is sleeping one night in the temple, when he is awakened by what he thinks is his godfather, Eli, calling him. He gets up and runs to his godfather's room to see what he wants. But the sleepy Eli has no idea what Samuel is talking about. He has been resting and can't remember saying a word. He sends the boy back to bed.

Then the same thing happens two more times. Eli realizes that either his godson is going nuts or something supernatural is happening. He wisely instructs Samuel that if it happens again he should answer the voice, "Speak, Lord, for Your servant is listening." The obedient Samuel runs back to bed to go to sleep. Sure enough, a fourth time the voice calls out. Samuel answers the voice just as he was told. Then the voice reveals Himself as the Lord, and He gives a message for Samuel to pass on to his godfather. It is clear here that the Lord is speaking in an audible voice to the young boy Samuel. It sounds to him just as if a person were calling him.

Throughout the Old Testament one can find many more examples of the Lord speaking in an audible voice. In the New Testament, we see God speaking in an audible voice several times as a testimony to Jesus being His Son. Also, we hear God speaking in an audible voice to Paul during his miraculous conversion (Acts 9:1-6). It is rare for God to speak in audible voice during the New Testament, but on rare occasions He still did.

I have never had this experience of God speaking to me in an audible voice. Most likely, you have not either. But I do know a few men and women who I respect that have had this happen, and it is a way God communicates with people a number of times in Scripture. However, from studying the New Testament and observing the way God works around me, I strongly believe this is not the normal way God communicates with us today. He tends to reserve it for times when He needs to do something dramatic to get our attention.

2. Dreams and Visions

Many times in both the Old and New Testaments we see God talking to people through dreams and visions. When Jesus is a young child, the evil King Herod tries to kill Him. But God warns Joseph, Jesus' father, in a dream to escape to Egypt. Joseph acts on his dream, and Jesus escapes the slaughter of babies ordered by Herod.

In Acts 9, God begins to speak to a man named Ananias through a vision. In that vision, Ananias and God have a conversation. God tells Ananias to go to a certain place and pray for a man there named Saul. Ananias obeys and finds the situation exactly as God had described. And the man Saul is waiting for him because Saul had received a vision in which a man named Ananias came to help him.

I had a friend in seminary who would sometimes receive information in dreams from the Lord. One time she had a dream about the secret sin of a pastor. She did not feel she could confront him on a dream, but she continued to pray for the situation. Soon enough, the pastor's sin surfaced and her dream was proved true.

Like an audible voice, this is not the typical way that God speaks to people today. However, that does not mean He never does. In fact, the Old Testament prophesies that when the Holy Spirit comes, "Your young men will see visions. Your old men will dream dreams." Frequently in the Scriptures, and still today, God speaks to His people in dreams and visions.

3. Exploding Scripture

After I finished college, I lived in a large city in Asia doing ministry among college students with my friend Matt. While I was there, one young man named Chan chose to follow Christ in a dramatic way. He was an electronics major who loved philosophy and had ambitions for politics. He was a voracious reader and liked the idea of being an intellectual. We had met with him several times to share the gospel and answer his questions about God. He believed all the facts about Jesus, but he was not yet willing to choose to follow Him. We lost contact with him for several weeks, but one day we ran into him on his college campus. His face lit up when he saw us, and he told us his story.

Several days before, something had happened that sent shockwaves throughout his life. A medical test revealed he had contracted an incurable disease. He had further testing done at the clinic to confirm the diagnosis. And then he went home. Sitting in his dorm room with a miserable future staring him down, he picked up his religion-major roommate's Bible off the shelf. Completely unfamiliar with the Bible, he opened to somewhere near the middle, looked down at the page, and read the first thing his eyes caught, "But I will restore you to health." He couldn't believe what he had just read. He blinked. He rubbed his eyes. But that promise was still staring right back at him.

He closed his Bible and opened it again to a different place. Again, the first thing he saw was a scripture promising healing. It seemed like the words were jumping off the page.

"This can't be for real," he thought to himself. One more time he shut his Bible and opened it. "I have heard your prayer and seen your tears; *I will heal you.*" He knew this was God speaking to him. That night he made a promise to God. If his medical tests came back with good news the next day, then he would follow God with his whole life. His heart felt a flood of peace that he had never before experienced. He went to sleep feeling better than he ever had. The next day he went back into the clinic to see the test results. They came back completely negative. He was healed. God was real. And Chan would serve Him for the rest of his life.

One of the most frequent ways I have experienced God speak to me is through what I call "exploding Scripture." Just like Chan, I will be flipping through the Scriptures or reading through a book of the Bible, and a verse will explode off the page with relevance to my life. Sometimes it will almost literally seem like the words are jumping off the page or bigger than everything else around them. These words may be an encouragement to me in a difficult situation I am facing, they may bring conviction of sin in life, or they may carry direction for a decision I must make. Whatever the application, I have an intense feeling that these words are specifically relevant to something in my life. The Scripture "explodes" off the page.

4. Fleece Test

The Bible tells a story where God calls a poor man named Gideon to lead the people of Israel in a revolt against the nation of Midian that was oppressing them. This is a ridiculous idea because the Midianites grossly outnumbered the people of Israel. So just to make sure that he had heard God right, Gideon asks the Lord to do something special for him. He would lay a fleece of lamb's wool out overnight, and when he awakes in the morning, he wants dew to be on the wool but not on the ground as a confirmation of what he is supposed to do. Gideon lays out the fleece that night. When he comes to check on it in the morning, he finds it exactly as he had asked.

But just to make sure this is not some bizarre coincidence, Gideon asks God that the next night when he lays out the fleece there would be dew on the ground but not on the fleece. Again, he awakes in the morning to find it just as he had specified. His courage bolstered by clarity of direction from God, Gideon boldly leads the Israelites into battle where they routed the enemy Midianites.

Sometimes today people will ask God to speak to them through circumstances just like Gideon did with the fleece. They will put out a bizarre or improbable condition to give God a chance to speak through circumstances. For example, my friend in college felt that God told him to go on a missions trip overseas one summer. However, it was going to cost a lot of money that he did not have. Also, the money for the plane ticket was due in less than a week. And it cost $1,400. So he said to God, "If You provide the money for the plane ticket by the due date, then I will take that as Your will to go on this trip." The next day he wrote a letter letting some friends know his need. He mailed the letter, knowing it would take at least two or three days before the letter even arrived to his friends. But six days later, he had every penny he needed for the plane ticket. God had met his fleece. He then did everything necessary to go on the trip and had a life-changing experience.

5. Message in Your Mind

A way that God will often speak to us is through a specific message in our minds. It is not an audible voice, but sometimes we will feel like we hear Him speaking to us in our heads. Maybe it will be a whole message or only one word, but it is a specific message from God to you. The story I told above about Jenna is a great example of a message in your mind. God did not speak aloud to me when I sat in my room, but He clearly spoke to me in my mind.

In Acts 21, the prophet Agabus comes to give a warning to the apostle Paul. He takes a cloth belt and ties Paul's hands together. Then he says, "The Holy Spirit says, 'In this way the Jews of Jerusalem will bind the owner of this belt and hand him over to the Gentiles.'" We do not read that Agabus heard an audible voice but he has a clear, specific message from the Lord. How did he receive this? Most likely, the Lord spoke it to him in his thoughts. In 1 Corinthians 14:26-33, the author mentions a "revelation coming to someone" during a church meeting and him sharing it with the rest of the church. Clearly, this is not an audible voice or there would be no need for the person to share the message. Rather, God is speaking a message into the mind of a believer.

Now, this is not an audible voice inside your head. It is also not necessarily a teleprompter message that flashes across your mind. Usually, God will speak to you in the context of your own thoughts. You will hear Him in your own inner voice, and you will have the sense that you are hearing from God.

6. Clear Sense of the Right Thing to Do

Sometimes God will give us a strong sense of what is the right thing to do. This is the most frequent way that God will give me direct communication. I do not feel any specific words in my mind, but I know just as clearly what choice I need to make.

Often I will have this feeling about sharing the gospel with others. One time I walked out of a restaurant at one in the morning to go home and get some sleep. As I walked through the parking lot to my car, I saw a group of five guys congregated around a pimped-out Civic. All of a sudden, I had a strong sense that I should tell them about Jesus. I shook it off, saying that it must be the food talking. And I got into my 12-year-old Toyota Corolla and started her up. Again, I felt clearly that I must share the truth with them. I couldn't ignore it now, so I began to make excuses in my head. I argued with myself in the car for a couple minutes. Then I shut my car off, and said, "Okay, God, I will obey."

I opened my door, walked over to them, and said, "Hey, guys. I was sitting in my car, and I felt like God told me to give you a message. I am really not insane. He actually told me He has an awesome plan for each one of your lives. And He loves you so much that He sent His Son Jesus to die on earth so that you could go to heaven." One of them looked back at me and said, "Hey. I go to church, too." And that opened the door to share the good news with the others for the next 15 minutes.

I did not hear specific words in my mind, but I knew beyond any doubt what God wanted from me because I had a clear sense of the right thing to do.

TESTING YOUR EARS

Now, as I am talking about hearing directly from God on this issue, some questions are probably popping into your head. How do I know it is really God speaking to me? Will God tell me to end a relationship? Will God tell me that I should marry someone? These are important questions because we can make horrible decisions if we are wrong about what we think God said. You can cause a lifetime of hurt and pain for yourself and others by acting on direction that did not really come from God. So let us look at some of those important questions.

How do I know it is God speaking to me?

Two important ingredients help us hear the word of God correctly. The first is experience. The more time you spend listening to God's voice, the more accurately you will be able to recognize it. If you want to hear God's voice clearly when it comes time to make an important decision, then you should be seeking to listen to His voice every day. This regular experience will make you much more adept at hearing Him when it is decision time.

The second ingredient is humility. See, no matter how much experience we have hearing the voice of God, we are still humans that make mistakes. Referring to our ability to supernaturally hear from God, 1 Corinthians 13:12 says, "Now we see but a poor reflection as in a mirror." Being a human on earth guarantees that we cannot hear God perfectly. We must be humble enough to admit this and test everything we think we hear from God. We should look at four tests each time we feel God has spoken something to us about making a decision.

Not so coincidentally, each of these is also a chapter in this book to test our decision in a marriage partner. I will talk about each of them in much more detail in those chapters.

The first test is Scripture. If what you feel God said to you does not line up with the teachings in the Bible, then you are wrong. End of story. The Bible is infallible. You are not. All direct communication must be submitted to the clear teachings of Scripture.

Inner peace is the second test. If you do not have a peace inside about the direction you think that God told you to go, then something is wrong. God is the source of our inner peace. If it is missing, then we should not move forward.

The third thing is we test our word from God against what our leaders think. We should seek the advice of our parents, pastors, and other spiritual leaders when we feel that God has spoken to us directly about a decision. If they do not agree with that direction, we should be humble enough to submit to the leadership that God put in our lives to protect us.

Finally, what our wise, Christian friends think serves as a test. Their opinion is not as crucial as what our leaders think, but it can be a source of great wisdom in testing what we feel we have heard from God.

I was planning to serve as a missionary in Asia for one year starting the fall after I finished graduate school. And the Lord provided a fantastic job for that summer. I would be able to work six months and save enough money to pay for my entire year overseas. It was an awesome opportunity.

Then I started reading a book about Hudson Taylor, the great missionary to China. He lived his entire life overseas without secular work or asking people for any money, he just trusted God. Continually, God would miraculously provide for Hudson and his whole organization. I wanted to live with radical trust like that. Then one day when I was praying, I felt like God said to give away all the money I was making that summer and He would provide for my trip.

I was scared. But I was also willing. I was going to give all that money away. What a step of faith. How exciting this would be.

I decided I should test this "word from God" before I did anything drastic. I checked the Bible. Jesus had told some people to give all their money away. This was definitely not something against the Bible. Then I told a good friend to see what he would think. He thought it was crazy, but he was excited about the idea. Two out of four, it looked like this faith step was actually going to happen.

But then I talked to my leaders. Without exception, they all told me they did not feel good about it. And the more I began to think about it, the more uneasy I felt, too. After some more prayer and counsel, I decided that this word was not from God, and I used the money from my job to serve the Lord in Asia. If I had gone ahead blindly without testing this word, I would have squandered the opportunity the Lord was giving me to serve Him in Asia.

If we are continually growing in our ability to hear God's voice and humble enough to test what we feel we hear, then we will remain safe from making destructive decisions because we misheard God. We do not need to fear mishearing God. We only need to test what we do hear.

Will God actually tell me not to marry someone?

My short answer is, "Yes!" Several times, I have felt God tell me unmistakably to either end a relationship or avoid a possible one. God wants us to be as useful and fulfilled as possible. The last thing

He wants is for you to be in a destructive relationship. He is going to help you avoid any relationship that will make it more difficult for you to serve Him. And He knows much better than we do how things will turn out.

We have a free will to walk into such a relationship if we choose, but He will try hard to stop us. He may choose to speak to us through any of the methods I mentioned in this chapter to warn us if we are walking in the wrong direction. The important thing is that we must be willing to obey no matter what the cost when God speaks to us. Our primary concern cannot be disappointing others, hurting our love, or being lonely. It must be obeying Jesus Christ. He must be our first loyalty; He must be our deepest love. We must be willing to break up with our girlfriend of several years. We must be willing to break off an engagement. Otherwise, our relationship is an idol, and it is certain to be a source of pain and problems in our lives.

Will God ever tell me that I should marry someone?

I don't have a short answer on this one. I think that some people may have genuine experiences of God telling them through direct communication that they should marry someone. And that is great. What a wonderful thing to know that God has ordained your marriage.

But here is my experience. Getting a direct word from God about who you should marry is an incredibly dangerous and unpredictable thing.

Two of my good friends in college began to date one fall. They were both passionate firebrands for Jesus. They were charismatic leaders, and people respected both of them for their ability to hear from God. Because I was friends with both of them, I was able to watch them both begin to fall for each other. I heard firsthand each dramatic spiritual experience where God spoke to them clearly that this was "the One" for them. If there was ever a relationship that God was speaking about, this was the one.

However, as a couple months went by, fighting and pain became the mark of their relationship. They were broken up by the end of the semester. As a friend, I looked at this mess of pain and disappointment and asked myself, "How can two godly people so mishear what God is saying?"

Two years later, I was home from graduate school over Thanksgiving break, and my girlfriend of a year broke up with me. I was crushed. I had been certain we would get married. I remembered sitting in my friend's car several months before telling him that God had told me in church that she was the one. As I lay awake in bed, I asked myself, "How could I have missed it so much? What did I do wrong?"

I could list another half-dozen friends who had "heard from God" only to see it end in disappointment. These are not unstable people. These are some of my Christian peers I respect the most, but they are befuddled when it comes to hearing God about relationships. Why?

Relationships stir up so many physical and emotional desires that our ability to hear from God often becomes clouded. It is wise to approach any sense that God is telling us to marry someone with tremendous caution.

If you feel like God tells you she is the one, then humbly put that message to the other tests contained in this book. If she lines up, that is a great confirmation of the relationship. If she does not line up, be humble and admit you might have heard wrong.

I just want to sum up this chapter for you. First, God speaks to us directly today and He may speak to you directly about your future marriage partner. Second, we must test that word against the Bible, our inner peace, our leaders, and our friends. Third, if God tells you to get out of a relationship, you must obey. Otherwise, you are heading for a world of pain. Finally, if you feel God told you to marry someone, be careful. Use that word as an encouraging confirmation, not a source of direction.

All of these principles are setting us up to hear correctly from God when He chooses to speak to us. However, the most important choice comes after we hear from God. We must choose to obey. That is the heart of the Obedience Test. No matter what else lines up, if God tells you, "No," then she is the wrong girl for you. You can't get around the issue. It is a very simple choice. Will I obey or will I choose my own way? And I'll give you a guarantee. If you disobey a clear direction from God on this one, you will regret it for the rest of your life.

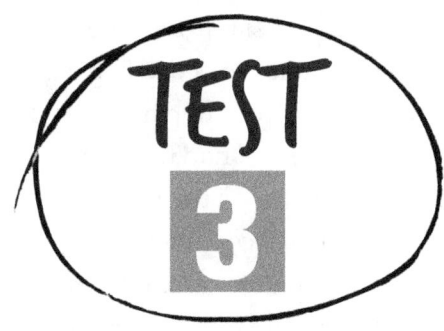

LEADERS TEST:
What do my key spiritual leaders think?

Ever since I was a teenager, I knew I wanted to buy a great engagement ring. My logic was if I hooked her up on the bling, then whenever I did something stupid she could just look at her left hand and everything would be okay. It would be like my get-out-of-jail-free card. But for this to work, I had to get my wife-to-be exactly what she wanted.

I was ready to spend big-time bucks… well, they were big-time bucks for me, at least. But first I had to figure out exactly what she wanted. I was going to hit a home run with this ring if it killed me.

To pull this off, I knew I needed some serious help. I didn't know the difference between white gold and platinum. I figured a princess cut must have been in the shape of a little girl. And, to make matters worse, my girlfriend had worked in a jewelry store.

If that weren't enough, I was living in Asia at the time so I couldn't see firsthand any of the rings in the States. I needed help bad.

So right away, I sent an email to her sister recruiting her to help. Then I got her two best friends in on the deal, too. I had them pumping her for information, while I researched rings on the internet.

I realized I needed some professional advice, too. So I began sending emails to all the jewelers I could find on the web. I told them what I knew she liked and asked for their input and recommendations.

I soon recognized I needed some experienced adults in on the deal, so I asked my mom and my girlfriend's mom to help me with stuff too. For every ring I found online, I would have her mom, sister, and friends check it out. For a period of a month, I had several emails going back and forth about the ring every day.

I knew that if I was going to do this right, I needed help. And thanks to a great set of guides, counselors, and advisors, I ended up getting a ring she absolutely loved.

I would never think of buying something as valuable as an engagement ring without getting the input of others who are more experienced than I am. Most of us will get advice from someone when it is time to pick out the ring. It may be from her friends, family, or maybe just the jeweler. But when making an expensive purchase where we have little experience, we know we need input from someone. The problem is some people do a better job getting advice in picking out the ring than they do in picking out the girl.

Besides following the clear teachings of the Bible and obeying the voice of God, I believe that the most pivotal factor in choosing a wife is the counsel of your spiritual leaders. The sad thing is that many young people skip this step altogether and pay the price later. No one has ever taught them the extreme importance of consulting their leaders when they make big decisions. This leaves them with a giant blind spot and an open door to foolish decisions.

WHO ARE MY SPIRITUAL LEADERS?

If their input is so important for making good decisions, I had better find out who my spiritual leaders are. Our spiritual leaders can be divided into three major categories.

1. Parents

Your parents are the primary spiritual authorities in your life. The Bible is chock full of exhortations to listen to and obey them. Proverbs 6:20-22 says, "My son, keep your father's commands and do not forsake your mother's teaching. Bind them upon your heart forever; fasten them around your neck. When you walk, they will guide you; when you sleep, they will watch over you; when you awake, they will speak to you".[14] The author says that the input of your parents is a guide, protector, and teacher. It will guide you as you navigate the difficult decisions of life. It will protect you from the devastating consequences that can come from choosing poorly. And it will teach you to make wiser decisions as you grow older.

He is not talking about little boys and girls here. He is saying that wherever you go, you should treasure the commands and teaching of your parents. Proverbs 13:1 says, "A wise son heeds his father's instruction, but a mocker does not listen to rebuke".[15] A good paraphrase might be, "If you want to be wise, listen to your dad; only an idiot ignores his parents' advice."

---

[14] See also Proverbs 1:8-9
[15] See also Proverbs 15:5

2. Pastors

The second group of spiritual leaders in your life is your pastors. Maybe your church only has one pastor; maybe it has hundreds. I am referring to those people who have a specific role in caring for you spiritually. That could be your youth pastor, young adults pastor, or senior pastor. Or maybe all of them. If you know wise men and women who hear from God and are interested in your life, why on earth would you not want their input into making the biggest decision in your life? You should be begging them to help you make a decision like this.

First Peter 5:5 reads, "You younger men, likewise, be subject to your elders."[16] This passage is not talking about showing respect to old folks. If you look at the previous four verses, you see that Peter is referring directly to the leaders of the church when he says "elders." The word translated as "be subject" means "to be put yourself under someone or be in obedience to someone." The least of that would be to seek their advice when making a major decision. God has placed these men in leadership for the express purpose of helping those they serve. The Lord has put your pastor in your life to help you succeed. His advice is a gift from heaven.

3. Mentors and Spiritual Advisors

Other significant spiritual leaders exist in our lives who are not parents or pastors. When it came time for me to propose, I was serving as a missionary overseas. As I began to think about taking the step of engagement, one of the people whose advice I sought

---

[16] NASB

was Kevin. He was the leader of my missions organization and a man I greatly admired. Wise and spiritually mature, he was exactly the kind of person whose advice I wanted. So I wrote him an email asking for his input before I made a final choice.

For you, it may be someone who helped lead you to the Lord or who first taught you about how to serve Jesus. Sometimes a teacher can fill this role in our lives. Many people have mentors who have played a significant role in their spiritual development. Our mentors and spiritual advisors can come in almost any shape. It is anyone you see as a spiritual leader to you. The Lord has given them a special role to speak into your life, and you should value their advice as a blessing from God.

WHY IS THEIR INPUT SO IMPORTANT?

Unarguably it is clear that the Bible tells us to seek the advice of our spiritual leaders. But why? I am sure our pastors and mentors have made mistakes. And we have seen our parents do things wrong for our whole lives. Why is their advice so special? Why does it make me a fool to ignore them? I can think of five reasons you would be an idiot to not ask for the input of your spiritual leaders.

1. One Is Not Enough

The Bible says repeatedly that one person is not enough to make a good decision. Wisdom comes from multiple perspectives. That way the incomplete viewpoints of yourself and your advisors can be combined to make wise choices. Proverbs 11:14 tells us, "For lack of guidance a nation falls, but many advisers make victory sure."[17] Victory is credited to having many advisors, and failure chalked up to not getting enough guidance. You need to seek the advice of your spiritual leaders simply to get multiple angles on the decision before you. Choosing a marriage partner is too difficult and dangerous a decision to attempt alone. Get help. The perspectives of others will give you more information to make a wise choice.

2. Wisdom of Experience

I am sure you have noticed that each of the three groups of leaders tends to be older than you. It is usually a big part of how they became your leader. With age comes opportunity for gaining wisdom and experience. Proverbs 20:29 says, "The glory of young men is their strength, gray hair the splendor of the old." Young men like us are not known for our wisdom. Our car insurance is twice as high as older adults for a reason. We have the special ability to be brave, strong, and powerful. Old men have lost the power of their youth, but they have replaced it with the wisdom from years of experience. In ancient Jewish culture, gray hair was a sign of the wisdom gained from many years of life. Our elders have experience that we have not yet been able to gain. If we are wise enough to learn from their experiences, then we have the head start of not having to learn each lesson on our own.

First Kings 12 tells the story of King Solomon's son Rehoboam. When Solomon died after a reign of tremendous prosperity and expansion for the nation of Israel, Rehoboam succeeded him as king. Immediately, the leaders among his people came to him and said,

---

[17] See also Proverbs 15:22; 24:6

"Your father worked us into the ground to build up the kingdom. Lighten our load and we will serve you for your whole life." Like a wise man, Rehoboam asked for three days to talk it over with his advisors. The people agreed. Rehoboam astutely asked for the advice for all the elders who had served his father before him. They advised him to do what the people asked to secure his kingdom during the transition of leadership.

Then Rehoboam met with many of his young friends to get their input. They counseled him to tell the people that he was twice the man his father was, and he would work them twice as hard if that's what he wanted. He was the king; they were the people. They could sit in the dungeon if they had a problem with it.

Somehow, in his youthful pride this seemed better advice to Rehoboam. When the people came back three days later, he ignored the advice of the elders and told them exactly what his friends had suggested. The people were outraged. They rejected him as king and angrily returned to their homes. Rehoboam confidently went with one of his officers to force them to work.

At this point, the crowds raged into an angry mob and stoned his officer. Rehoboam barely escaped by chariot back to his palace. That day ten of the twelve tribes in his kingdom seceded. For the rest of his days there was war and destruction in Israel. His greatly weakened kingdom was later attacked by Egypt and plundered of all the incredible wealth his father had amassed. Rehoboam was left with only the shattered remains of a once great kingdom and a lifetime to regret having ignored his elders' advice.

Do not despise the counsel of those older than you. They have seen much more of life than you have. Trust their experience and wisdom over your own.

3. Blessing of God

Because all of our authority figures and spiritual leaders are established by God, when we obey and submit to them, we are in a very real way directly obeying and submitting to God. And He promises to bless us for that. Because God has established our authority, He will use it in our lives. It is one of His favorite tools to guide us.

Ephesians 6:1-3 says, "Children, obey your parents in the Lord, for this is right. 'Honor your father and mother'–which is the first commandment with a promise–'that it may go well with you and that you may enjoy long life on the earth.'" If we honor our parents, God promises us a long, prosperous life. This is one example of God's promise that when we honor our spiritual leaders, it brings blessing and protection to our lives.

Romans 13:2-3 says, "Consequently, he who rebels against the authority is rebelling against what God has instituted, and those who do so will bring judgment on themselves." This verse refers specifically to the government but is true of leadership figures in general. Just as to obey our spiritual leaders is like obeying God and brings blessing, to disobey them is to rebel against God and brings judgement.

Our parents, pastors, and other leaders have been sovereignly inserted by God into our lives to guide us and protect us from foolish decisions. Because He has put them in that capacity, they have a special ability from Him to be able to help us. And we receive a special blessing from Him if we are willing to submit to them.

4. Outside the Situation

Another thing that makes the advice of your spiritual leaders so valuable is that they are outside of the situation. One time I was driving down the highway in my 12-year-old Toyota Corolla, and I heard a "Clunk!" This was not an ordinary clunk, but the car kept going so I just went on driving. All of a sudden I noticed the driver of the car behind me was blinking his high beams at me. I checked my speedometer. I was going fast enough. What was his problem?

Then the car proceeded to accelerate into the passing lane and pulled up alongside of me. The passenger in the car was frantically waving her arms out the window and shouting. She was really upset. "What on earth did I do?" I wondered to myself. I couldn't read her lips, so I began to roll down the window. When it opened enough so I could stick my head out, I did catch her words.

"Your car is on fire! Your car is on fire! Get out before it explodes!"

I looked behind me. I couldn't see anything. And there was no smoke coming from the hood. But the look on her face clearly said that she was not joking, so I quickly pulled over. As I jumped out of the car, I saw the whole bottom of my car was in flames. I had been shooting down the highway with a flame trail like a comet.

I had a serious problem as I was driving that day, but I had no idea. Many of the warning signs I could not see; and the warning sign I did hear, I didn't know how to interpret. I needed the perspective of someone outside of the situation.

In any situation, it is helpful to have the viewpoint of those who can look at the issue through fresh eyes. They are not burdened with the emotional baggage of the situation; they can look at the circumstances objectively. How much more important is this in a relationship where your emotions are going crazy.

5. Don't Need to Please You

A great thing about your spiritual leaders is that they do not need to please you. That is not always true with our friends. Our friends place great importance on our relationship, and sometimes they will not say something that is important but could be difficult and hurtful. Your spiritual leaders tend to be more willing to say what you need to hear regardless of how it makes you feel. They care more about your best interests than they do about the relationship.

We see this difference in the Rehoboam story from 1 Kings 12. After the elders gave him their wise advice, the Bible says, "Rehoboam rejected the advice the elders gave him and consulted the young men who had grown up with him and were serving him."[18] The young king rejected his elders' advice from the outset. He did not even wait until he heard any other options. I am sure at this point his friends are probably thinking, "Let's just tell him what he wants to hear." And they gave him the advice that ended up destroying his kingdom.

Could they really have thought it was good advice to threaten his subjects? Even if he needed them to keep doing forced labor, he could have at least made a compromise or said it nicely. No, they were his childhood friends who had gotten royal jobs as a favor. They needed to please him. So they told him what he wanted to hear. Meanwhile the elders, who were courageous enough to tell the king the truth, were ignored.

---

[18] 1 Kings 12:8

WHAT SHOULD I DO?

The first responsibility you have in getting the input of your spiritual leaders is to seek out their advice. Do not wait for them to come to you. Ask them for their opinions. Their counsel is precious. If you knew there was a treasure buried nearby, would you sit at home and hope that somehow it appeared in your room one day? No! You would immediately go out and start digging. Treat your leaders' thoughts like a treasure. Go looking for their advice.

Proverbs 20:18 exhorts us, "Make plans by seeking advice; if you wage war, obtain guidance." It is the one who wants a successful war who will take the initiative. He seeks the advice; he obtains the guidance. If you are wise enough to value the advice of your leaders, you will take the initiative to get their input. Only a fool will not consult the wise.[19]

Seeking their advice, however, is not enough. Proverbs 19:20 says, "Listen to advice and accept instruction, and in the end you will be wise."[20] We must go beyond seeking their advice to listening to and accepting it. If we truly understand the power of their advice, we will apply it to our lives.

During college, I was on the verge of beginning a relationship with a girl from my church. We had been friends for years, and we were right on the cusp of becoming something more. One night during that time, I was at a church service. During the meeting, one of the church leaders came up to me and told me that as he was praying for me, he felt God tell him something to share with me. He said, "God will order your steps. So be careful of the relationships you let into your life. Be careful of your romantic involvements, because the Lord has someone special He wants to team you up with."

---

[19] See Proverbs 15:12
[20] See also Prov. 15:31

That wasn't quite what I was expecting to hear. Later that night I was sitting on the porch with my almost girlfriend, and I told her what the pastor had said. After a long silence she replied, "Toby, I think we need to back off our relationship after hearing what that minister said tonight. We need to take time to carefully weigh what he had to say to you." I casually shrugged my shoulders and, without ever processing his input, said, "Nah! I feel right about this. I think he must have been wrong this time." A few weeks later we started a relationship. Unsurprisingly, it didn't work out.

Proverbs 13:13 says, "He who scorns instruction will pay for it, but he who respects a command is rewarded." I scorned a wise man's word from God, and we both suffered for it. Listen to your leaders' advice. Receive the reward that comes from respecting their counsel. Please learn from the hurt I walked through for my foolishness. Do not repeat the same mistake.

BUT WHAT IF...?

1. What if I disagree?

What I am saying to you might sound crazy or it might sound smart, but either way you are probably asking yourself a couple questions. The first of which is, "What if I disagree? Is there never anytime where I might be right and they might be wrong?"

In most situations, if you listen to their counsel and prayerfully consider what your leaders are saying, then I believe that you will come to see that they are right. But rare instances exist where even after thinking and praying about it you still have differing opinions.

In this case, I would suggest that you make an appeal to your spiritual leaders. Sit down with them and honestly and respectfully share why you disagree. Ask them if they could support your way of doing things. Perhaps your leaders will respond by seeing your way as a good choice. But what if they maintain that your way is a poor choice?

If after prayerfully considering their counsel and respectfully explaining your point of view disagreement between you and your spiritual leaders still exists, then you basically have two different courses you can take. You can respectfully disagree and graciously choose what you think is right. Or you can go against your own instinct and choose to follow their advice instead.

Although it may seem crazy, I think the second option is the better one. The counsel of our leaders is so powerful that it is worth choosing even when we disagree. Proverbs is pretty clear about how much we should trust the way that seems right to us. In 14:12 says, "There is a way that seems right unto a man, but in the end it leads to death." Your feelings about what is right are a poor judge of the correct path. You can feel right walking down the road all the way until you fall off the cliff.

Proverbs 12:15 says it even more clearly, "The way of a fool seems right to him, but a wise man listens to advice." As painful as it might seem, a wise man listens to advice over what seems right to him. He is a fool who chooses his feelings over advice. This is a difficult pill to swallow. We want to believe that our instincts are good. But the Bible teaches us that our instincts are not the path to a wise decision.

Another proverb gives us insight into why we should choose the advice of others over what seems right to us. Proverbs 16:30 says, "Whoever gives heed to instruction prospers, and blessed is he who trusts in the LORD." Often the two-line poetry of the Proverbs will say the same thing in two different ways. For example, Proverbs 12:28 says, "In the way of righteousness is life; along that path is immortality." The "way of righteousness" equals "the path." And "life" equals "immortality."

It is the same in this verse. "Prosper" equals "blessed." And "gives heed to correction" equals "trusts in the Lord." Wait. It does?

Choosing to listen to your leaders over your own gut is an act of trusting God. He established those leaders over you, and He tells you to submit to them. When you obey Him against what seems right to you, you are putting your trust in Him. You are choosing His way over your way, and His blessing is found on that path.

2. What if my spiritual leaders counsel me contrary to what the Bible teaches?

This is the extremely rare exception when it may be necessary to not follow the input of a spiritual leader. For example, if your pastor asks you to lie to cover a mistake he made, you should not lie. The Bible is your authority before your pastor. Or if your parents tell you to renounce your faith in Christ, you cannot do this. Christ is your authority before your parents. But these are extremely rare situations.

And in the context of finding a marriage partner, no biblical commands tell you to marry anyone in particular. So, if your spiritual leaders give you counsel against proceeding with a certain girl, you cannot claim the Bible as your excuse for refusing their advice.

3. What if my parents aren't Christians?

If your parents are not Christians, then it can seem odd to have their advice guiding you as you try to follow Jesus. Similarly, you might think your parents are not wise or good decision-makers, even if they are Christians. This makes it confusing to try to make good decisions.

The most important thing to remember is that they are still the God-appointed authority in your life if they are believers or not. The commands in the Bible to obey and honor your parents do not have the qualifier "if they are Christians" in them. We should honor and obey our parents because they have been given to us by God, not because they are godly and wise. So in everything we do we must honor them, and if they give us a command that does not directly conflict with obeying God, then we are to obey it.

Also, I believe that 90% of the time our parents' advice will be good simply because they have more experience. However, their advice will be tainted if they are not Christians by their wrong set of beliefs. If they are simply offering their opinions and not asking you to take a specific course of action, compare their advice against all your other leaders. Does everyone else disagree with them? Then you should ask your parents if they would feel dishonored if you chose to go against their advice. If they are okay with that, then you can feel released to follow the advice of your Christian leaders over that of your parents. This is an incredibly rare set of circumstances, and this course should only be taken if you can still honor and obey your parents while not accepting their advice.

4. What if my godly leaders are giving me different advice?

A confusing situation erupts when you begin to get conflicting advice from your godly leaders. You do not know whose advice to apply. The first thing you should do is go back to your different leaders and let them know about the different advice you are getting. If you do this, the situation will usually resolve itself. Maybe one leader will change his mind or will voluntarily submit his advice to another's counsel. Your father might tell you to listen to your pastor after hearing his advice. Or maybe your mentor will tell you it is best to listen to your parents. This is almost always what will happen. The conflict of opinions simply resolves itself.

If a disagreement of counsel is not settled by that, a rank order of authority exists between these three different categories. First is your parents. They bear the ultimate responsibility in training you to make good decisions, and the Bible is the most clear about the need to honor, obey, and submit to them. Second is your pastors. They have also been formally established by God as a spiritual authority in your life. Third is mentors and other spiritual advisors. Their spiritual leadership in your life is real, but it is more informal and secondary.

If you are absolutely forced to make a decision between two different counsels from godly persons, I would choose according to that ranking system. Your parents are to be heeded above the others, and your pastor should be listened to before a more informal spiritual leader. The good news is you will probably never have to make that choice.

WATCHMAN TEST:
Do I feel God's peace about this relationship?

I am not good at making new friends. So my first week at Bible school was a little intimidating. But during registration, a wonderful thing happened. This tall, blond, beautiful girl came up and started talking to me.

I was a little nervous because I did not often find myself in the company of beautiful girls who wanted to talk to me. But she made it so natural. She knew how to make a conversation fun.

The next day she came up and sat next to me at lunch. We talked and joked and got to know each other better. She was a total blast to be around. Pretty soon, we were sitting together in the front row of all our classes. We would eat most of our meals together. She would ask me to help her study in the library.

She had a unique ability to flirt with a guy and make him feel like he was the man. Using words or a gentle touch, she could communicate that you were special to her. After a few weeks I realized that I was beginning to enjoy her company in a special way.

Just as my heart was beginning to turn toward her, I started to have another feeling inside, too.

Inner turmoil.

I felt very uneasy about the relationship. When I thought of us being something more than friends, I was excited about the idea. But I also felt an elusive discomfort about the whole thing. I had no peace in my heart.

As time went by, it became clear to me that something was wrong, and I needed to back off in this friendship. I began to pull away. I sat other places in class, met other friends for lunch, and was busy when she wanted to study. I knew something wasn't right, but I didn't know what.

As I pulled away, another guy began to fill the same role in her life. They began to spend all their time together. I had been replaced.

That was painful. I knew I had initiated the whole separation, but I still did not know why. I just didn't feel right about the whole thing.

At Christmas break, she and her new friend were caught sleeping together at the local hotel. Both of them were kicked out of Bible school, and their future plans were shattered. They didn't even stay together. It was all a waste.

And when I heard all that happened, I immediately knew that could have been me. My inner uneasiness had saved me from a tragedy.

God will often communicate with us through a lack of inner peace. Philippians 4:6-7 says, "Do not be anxious about anything, but in everything, by prayer and petition, with thanksgiving, present your requests to God. And the peace of God, which transcends all understanding, will guard your hearts and your minds in Christ Jesus."

This passage teaches us that we do not need to worry about problems or big decisions in our lives. Instead, we talk to God about them, and then let His peace protect us.

His peace "transcends all understanding." I often thought this meant that His peace is so great we can't even grasp it. But as I studied this passage I realized, while that is true, I don't think it is what the author is trying to say. He is saying, "His peace is superior to our understanding." His peace is a better guard than our understanding. All our plans and research and thought are inferior to the guidance we can get from following His peace. Our understanding is informed by our limited knowledge. But the peace of Christ is built on the full knowledge of God. He knows the future, and He knows what is in other people's hearts. His peace is a far superior guide than our limited understanding.

For example, one time I was purchasing a plane ticket to Asia. Now, I like to think I am a good shopper, especially on the internet. So I set out to get a great deal. I compared prices at all the travel websites. I sent emails out to a dozen travel agents. I searched on websites dedicated to Asian travel. I tried to work with some international travel agents just to see if I could gain an advantage off the currency exchange. After all that research, I discovered that I was a little late in buying the ticket so I would have to pay $150 more than the best price. And even that price would be gone soon. The prices were going up every day as the cheapest tickets were being bought. I had to act soon.

When I went to buy the ticket, I had an offer from a travel agent that was $50 cheaper than anything else available. But I had this slightly uncomfortable feeling inside. My peace was disturbed.

I needed to get it soon, so I went ahead and bought it. Only a few hours later I received an email from a travel agent who had not gotten back to me for days. She offered me a better ticket for $150 cheaper.

God's peace was superior to my understanding. After hours and hours of research, I still did not know enough to make the correct choice. But God did. And He led me in the right direction with His peace. I was just too foolish to listen.

Philippians goes on to say that this peace will "guard your hearts and your minds in Christ Jesus." The Greek word translated "guard" is a military term from that day. It refers to posting a sentinel to keep watch and protect a city from invasion. It is the watchman, the person who is the first to see if trouble is approaching.

It is not a troop of guards that stands at the gate and protects the city. It is one man. And as one man he does not have the ability to defend the city. All he can do is warn the city. If one night he is standing guard and in the distance he sees an enemy approaching, he will immediately begin to warn the others. He might ring a bell or blow a horn or shout at the top of his lungs. He will do whatever it takes to alert the others. Then it is the army's responsibility to defend the city.

Your peace acts like that guard. When something is trying to invade your heart and mind that is not right, he begins to jump and shout to warn you. Inside you begin to feel unsettled. Then you know it is time to protect yourself from a bad decision. God's peace warns you, but it does not protect you. You must be willing to listen to that sentinel and respond.

What would happen if when that guard was blowing his horn to alert the city, the army decided to ignore him and keep sleeping? The enemy would attack, and the one guard could do nothing to protect the city. The city would be completely destroyed because the people did not heed the warning.

Often the same thing happens to many of us. The Holy Spirit tries to warn us of impending problems through removing His peace, but we pay no attention to His cry. Just like I did when I bought the plane ticket, we ignore the warning. Then as we stumble into relationship problems and pain, we wonder how we could have avoided it all. Listen to the watchman.

We must take an important step to activate God's peace in our lives. Before Philippians 4 talks about the greatness of God's peace in verse 7, it gives an important command in verse 6. It says, "Do not be anxious about anything, but in everything, by prayer and petition, with thanksgiving, present your requests to God." The protective peace of God is activated by prayer.

Prayer is the stationing of the watchman. It puts the warning system in place. When I face a difficult decision in a relationship, I talk to God about it. I present my request to Him, and *then* His peace guards my heart and mind. It is not that the Holy Spirit will refuse to warn or help us if we do not pray first. But prayer puts us in the posture of trusting the Lord for protection. It puts the trumpet in the hand of the guard so that we can easily hear his warning. It is crucial to take time to pray when you are facing a relationship decision. This not only helps you hear from the Lord at the moment you are praying, but also positions peace to protect you as you walk through the process of making the decision.

If you feel uncomfortable inside about making a decision, then it does not matter what else you want or think. You need to wait.

Take more time to pray about it and see if you feel that peace return to your spirit. If it does not, then your guard is trying to tell you something. The Holy Spirit is trying to talk to you through this lack of peace. Be willing to listen.

KEEPING THE PEACE

Lack of inner peace is often an ambiguous feeling. It is a divine discomfort that you might not be able to put your finger on. Because of this, I have found three practices to be extremely helpful in discerning whether His peace is with me or not.

1. Quiet the Noise

Many times we have difficulty hearing the shouts of our watchman over the noise of life. Our mind is so busy with other thoughts and our heart so busy with other feelings, that our disturbed peace is not even noticed. We need to quiet the noise so that we can listen to our peace.

When I face a big decision, I will often go into my bedroom or another quiet place to spend time thinking and praying about it. I process all my thoughts and feelings by writing them down until my mind runs out of things to say. Then I try to be quiet inside and just ask myself the one question, "Do I feel right about this?" In that place of inner quietness, my ability to hear the Peace Alert is greatly enhanced.

2. Remove the Pressure

Another key to experiencing the protection of God's peace is to remove yourself from decision pressure. In the story about my airline ticket purchase, I mentioned that I felt a lot of pressure to buy the tickets quickly. When you make a decision in this environment, it is easy to ignore the subtle warnings of God's peace. If faced with a high pressure moment, refuse to give a decision until you have time to quiet yourself and listen. Even if it seems like you might lose out, delay the decision and listen to what God's peace is saying. Hearing from God is important enough to risk losing out on some opportunities. You will definitely come out ahead in the end if you have the input of the Lord of the Universe on a consistent basis.

3. Fake the Decision

To help myself understand what I am actually feeling about a situation, I will pretend to actually make the decision. Then I will evaluate what feelings that evoked in me. For example, you are thinking about proposing to your girlfriend. You have been dating for a few years, and it seems like it is time to take the next step toward marriage. She is a great girl, and your friends, parents, and pastors are all in favor of you proposing. But you know this is a *huge* decision, so you want to test God's peace in your heart.

If I were you, I would go to a quiet place. Then I would say, "Yes, I am going to do it. I am going to ask her to marry me." Then I would immediately check how that made me feel. Did I feel uneasy? Afraid? Or just plain excited? Then I would say, "No, I am not asking her to marry me." Did that make me feel relieved or disappointed? Making these mock decisions can help stir up what I am feeling so that it is easier to perceive. If a mock decision arouses all kinds of fear, doubt, and discomfort, then my inner peace is probably trying to tell me something.

God's gift of guarding peace is one of the most powerful aids we have in making good decisions. We are being foolish if we do not listen to the feedback from God trying to keep us from pain and problems. So as you take steps forward in your relationships, always check to see if the peace in your heart is disturbed. If that watchman is making noise, it is because trouble is on the horizon.

FRIENDS TEST:
What do my closest friends think?

You are a poor judge of whether a girl you like will make a good wife for you. Let me repeat that. You are a poor judge of whether a girl you like will make a good wife for you. You are blinded by infatuation. Praise God for the intoxicating joy of attraction, but it renders you stupid. It really does.

One of my friends was eating lunch at a table in his college's cafeteria with a bunch of friends, including the girl he had a crush on. Midway through the meal, the group's conversation turned to what made someone of the opposite sex attractive. Each person in the group took a turn sharing what physical characteristics made a girl or guy appealing to him. There were all the usual answers for mixed company – deep eyes, a slender figure, big muscles, and long hair. When it finally came turn for the girl to share her desires, my friend had his pen out ready to take notes. She said, "I am actually attracted to guys that are a little chubby. I love a nice little belly on a man." My friend immediately went to work on his figure. By the end of the semester, he had purposely gained over 20 pounds.

We do stupid things when we are in love. So how do I protect myself, if I am blinded by the very relationship I need to inspect? You get the input of people who can still see clearly. Your friends. They are not in love with your girl. At least I hope not. If they are, then you need to get some new friends.

Now, I am not talking about just any friends. If you have ever been in a relationship, then you know that everyone has opinions about it. And many of them are wrong. A specific kind of qualified friend makes it to the panel for the Friends Test.

First, they are **believers**. If your friends are not Christians, then they do not possess the perspective and values that are necessary to help you choose a good wife. They may be smart or even wise, but their lives are built on a different foundation. Their goals and directions in life will not take them or you toward God's will.

Second, they are **wise**. Many well-meaning Christians out there make horrible decisions with their lives. If they can't make good decisions themselves, why on earth do you want them to help you? You want the perspective of friends who have the evidence of consistently making wise, godly decisions in their own lives. They have the ability to hear from God in a situation and discern what a wise decision would be. Wise friends are like gold. Treasure them.

Third, they are **close** to you. Although nothing is wrong with getting the counsel from wise acquaintances, what you really want is the advice of close friends. People who know the girl and have seen both of you together. They will know what kind of girl is good for you. Your wife should not only be a great person, but she should have a great effect on you. Close friends have a sixth sense for long-term compatibility.

What these friends think about your potential mate is important for several reasons. First, if you marry someone that your friends do not like, then you are probably going to lose some of your friends. Hopefully, all your boys will not desert you as soon as you tie the knot. But how excited do you think they will be to see you if you are now one flesh with someone they don't like? Most likely, you will see these close relationships drift away if you become one with someone they don't want to be around.

Second, your friends are probably a lot like you. You share at least some common experiences, interests, values, and perspectives. That is doubtless why you became friends in the first place. Now, I do not think the mysteries of love can be solved with simple logic. But it stands to reason that if your friends do not like her, then when the infatuation wears off, you might not like her too much either. This is not an absolute rule because we are not exactly like our friends. But it should make you take a huge pause if your friends are not too keen on her.

Finally, your friends can see things that you can't. This is why their input is so valuable. They are outside the situation and the romance so they can see clearly. A big reason for this is the blinding effect of love I mentioned earlier. You become totally oblivious to major character flaws. Her bad habits that are downright annoying to everyone else in the world are cute to you. Basically, you think she is a way better person than she really is.

God knew that no one would get married if their initial views of each other were of all their flaws. So He created attraction and infatuation to cover flaws during the initial stages of love. However, infatuation is so effective at covering problems that it limits our ability to make wise decisions on our own. The input of your friends (and leaders) helps you come to terms with any major problems that attraction has hidden from you.

ASKING FOR ADVICE

Several years ago, I was sitting in my apartment talking to one of my closest friends. He was sitting on the bed, and I was leaning back in my computer chair. And as close friends often do, we were talking about girls. Actually, to be exact, we were talking about past girlfriends. We were lamenting the errors we had made in the past and wondering how on earth we had missed all the warning signs.

In the middle of this regretful reminiscing, my friend turned to me and said, "Toby, how could you have let me get into that relationship?"

I looked at him in disbelief. I had cautioned him many times about this relationship, but he had never listened. I reminded him of this and jogged his memory with some specific examples.

In the silence that followed, I leaned back further in my black computer chair and thought to myself about how good a friend I was. I almost always shared concerns I had with my friends. I thought about all the times I had turned out to be right. Then all of a sudden a thought hit me. Why don't my friends ever look out for me? How come they never warn me before I make a mistake? What kind of friends do I have that let me walk blindly into pain and hurt?

These thoughts erupted into words as I blurted, "Hey! How come you never warn me before I make a mistake? Where were you when I was getting ready to date *my* last girlfriend?"

My friend returned the same look I flashed a moment before. He retorted, "Toby, I did tell you. What are you talking about?"

And he went on to cite the exact situation. Then both of us sat in silence, realizing how much pain we could have avoided in life if only we had listened to each other.

How could we have missed a clear warning from a best friend? Many times, one guy will feel like he shared his concerns with his friend, but the friend never really heard him. The secret to seeking your friends' advice is that when they do share it, you must be ready to listen.

Before you get into a relationship or take a significant step forward in any relationship you have, here is an acronym for what you should do with each of your good friends. Ask for their A-D-V-I-C-E.

A - Affirm the Friendship

Your first concern is to make sure your friend feels comfortable sharing his thoughts with you. It can be an intimidating thing to talk badly about the love of one of your close friends. Many people in the world have ended friendships over such things. Make sure he feels that no matter what he says, your friendship will not suffer. He must feel safe if you want to get his true thoughts.

D - Drag it Out

Even after reassuring him that you want to know his honest opinion, it will still take some effort to get it out of him. It is a scary situation for him to be in. What if he takes a strong stand against you dating her and you end up dating her anyway? Now, he feels like a jerk whenever he hangs out with you two. You might need to drag his honest thoughts out of him. The secret to doing this is by asking specific questions.

Before you talk to him, have a list ready of questions you want to ask him to find out what he really thinks. He will most likely not want to volunteer bad thoughts about the situation. But if you ask him directly, a good friend won't lie to you.

Some questions you might ask are: Do you think she makes me a better person? Are you happy that we are together? Do you see any major problems in her character? Do you like being around us when we are together? Would you be comfortable if we were getting married?

If he answers a question with an overwhelmingly positive response, then move on. But if he answers you with a negative or tentative response, dig deeper. Ask follow-up questions like the following: What do you mean by that? You don't sound too confident; how come? Can you tell me more about that? Try to drag out anything negative he might feel about the relationship.

V - Value His Thoughts

This conversation might be hard. You are asking him to say negative things about a girl you might already be in love with. Something will rise up inside you that wants to disagree with every negative thing he says. You will want to fight back and defend her. Don't give in to that. Just be quiet and listen.

Proverbs 27:6 says, "Wounds from a friend can be trusted, but an enemy multiplies kisses." You can trust a true friend even when he is hurting you because you know he is for your best interests. The words of a friend are like a doctor's scalpel. They only cut to bring healing. Would you attack the doctor who comes at you with a scalpel? No. You know that he will only hurt you if it is for your good. The words of friends are the same way.

To be a good friend and a wise man, you need to value your friend's thoughts. Do not attack them. Count each apprehension he shares as a significant thing. He is being vulnerable to share these concerns with you. And he is doing it because you asked. Not only are these thoughts valuable because it is your friend sharing them, but they should be precious to you as input for making a good decision. If you flippantly disregard what a close friend shares with you, you are being a fool and a bad friend.

I - Identify His Specific Concerns

During the initial conversation you should try to get a summary of any concerns that your friend has. If it doesn't make you feel too weird, have a pen and paper with you. When you feel like you understand a specific concern or a theme of concerns that he is sharing, repeat it back to him. If he acknowledges that you got what he meant, then write it down. Do this until you feel that you have a grasp of each concern that he has shared.

C - Communicate your Appreciation

As you close this specific conversation, it is crucial that you express how much you appreciate your buddy being open with you. Acknowledge that it may have been difficult, but tell him how important his opinions are to you. Let him know that you want him to come to you if he has any more concerns about the relationship in the future.

E - Explore Each Concern

After the conversation or in the days that follow, you should take time to explore each issue that your friend brought up. Do some soul searching. Be honest with yourself. Is your friend right? Take time to pray over each thing he brought up. You can use these concerns to help ask good questions to leaders and other friends. Then you can see if it is just your one friend or if everyone feels the same.

Remember, "Oil and perfume make the heart glad, so a man's counsel is sweet to his friend" (Proverbs 27:9). The advice of a friend should be as sweet as perfume. It comes from love and is consumed with your best interests. He can see things that you cannot. His advice can protect you and help you choose a wife who will bless your life.

CARPOOL TEST:
Are we going to the same place?

When I was fresh out of high school, I went to a Bible school in western New York called Elim Bible Institute. Elim is a place of spiritual growth like nowhere else I have ever encountered. But love for God is not the only thing that flourishes there.

I have this theory that each year Cupid saves up all his most potent arrows and then just goes crazy at Elim. Despite the best efforts of the school to keep its students focused, a higher percentage of people fall in love there in a three-year period then just about any other place in the world.

Because of this, Elim has developed a sort of legendary reputation. People call it Elim Bridal Institute. Some say, "Elim is like a shoe factory; they fix your souls (soles), lace up your tongue, and send you out in pairs." The joke motto for the women is, "Ring by spring or your money back." So I figured that with all these expectations, I should be looking around at least.

I guess you need to know two things about me before I go on. One is that I want to spend my life working with young adults because I believe that no other group can make a greater impact for the kingdom of God. The second thing is that I always want the best. I don't like to settle for mediocrity. So I found the most beautiful girl in the entire school and said, "I am going after her."

Now this girl was beautiful, like cover-of-the-magazines-next-to-the-candy-at-the-grocery-store beautiful. She was way out of my league. For her to end up with me would have been like a supermodel falling for… well, me. I had hung out with her in groups a few times, but I never even talked with her one-on-one.

Then one day I walked into our overcrowded cafeteria and, as I looked for a seat, I saw her alone at a table. It was like a spotlight was shining down from heaven, and the angelic choir was singing the "Hallelujah Chorus." I took this as a clear sign from God, so I sat down next to her as smoothly as I possibly could. And we began to talk. Not only was she stunningly gorgeous, but she was intelligent and witty with an all-around great personality. This was too good to be true.

I decided to pull out the ultimate Christian pickup line. I hope you have a pen and paper because this is worth the price of the book right here.

I said, "So… what do you feel called to do with your life?"

She looked at me with her enchanting, Little Mermaid-sized green eyes, and a smile revealed her perfect, white teeth.

Fireworks were going off. An entire orchestra was playing for me.

I could hear the wedding bells right there.

She smiled, looked me in the eye, and said, "I want to work with old people my whole life."

The fireworks disappeared; the orchestra ground to a halt. I nodded my head a couple times to take in what just happened.

Then I said, "Oh, that's great," without meaning it at all.

After a polite end to the conversation, I excused myself and walked away, knowing it could never work.

Sometimes you'll meet a great girl, but you find out she is going somewhere different in life than you are. You want to work with college students, and she wants to work with senior citizens. You want to live a relaxed life even if you are poor, but she wants to be rich. You want to stay near home, but she wants to be a missionary. You want to start a relationship now, but she wants to wait until after med school. Is there a way to reconcile those differences? Or is God's plan keeping you apart?

If life is a journey, then marriage is sharing a car on that trip. The fact is you will find many great people in the world that you could love, but you could never share a car. Perhaps they are going to a different destination or they are taking a different route to get there. Maybe they just want to go a different speed or they like a different style of car. Whatever the reason, it is not a natural carpool. With each difference, you have a choice. You can either compromise in the area of difference to be with this person, or you can keep your travel plans and travel separately.

It may seem right to give up something as small as travel plans for love; but if we are going to be complete, we must have some values we are not willing to compromise. If God has called you to be a missionary, I sure hope you wouldn't sell that out for a girl. Other things, however, are acceptable to compromise. Maybe she loves you so much she will be willing to live a life where she does not have much money. That is a difficult choice, but it is her choice to make. Ultimately, it is your choice how much you are willing to compromise to share a car with your wife. But wisdom would say that the journey will be much more enjoyable if you are both happy about the direction you are traveling.

There are three categories of differences that can keep two people from sharing a car... and a man and woman from sharing a life.

1. Different Destinations

If two people want to go to two different destinations, then they cannot share a car on the journey. No matter how great we get along, we can't share a car if I want to go to California and you want to go to New York. Either we have to split up or one of us has to change his destination. The same is true in life. If I want to be a successful businessman and my girlfriend wants to be a pastor's wife, we have a problem. Either we will go our separate ways or one of us won't get what we want.

Recently one of my best friends was interested in an awesome girl who had strong feelings for him as well. I knew both of them and what they wanted in life. He had a passion for stirring up young people in America to give their lives for God. She wanted to spend her life as a missionary in Northern Africa. I can't think of two better things to do with your life, but they don't easily work together. I shared this with my friend, and he had already decided that it could not work for that reason. He thought she was great, but she could not be the one for him unless something changed in one of their hearts.

It was the same with the girl in the story at the beginning of the chapter. In many ways, she was everything a guy could ever wish for. But she was going somewhere different than I was, and I was not willing to compromise my destination for the passenger.

Each of us has plans and dreams for the future. Some of those are things God has spoken to us, some are things that are treasured desires, and some are mere hopes or wishes we hold. Giving up your God-given direction in life for a girl is wrong. That is prioritizing your girl over God. And that is idolatry. No matter how great she seems, she is not worth selling out your faith.

Perhaps you would be willing to sacrifice other parts of your destination. You always wanted to be a CIA agent, but you are willing to give up that dream to settle down with a wife. That is your choice. There is no clear-cut right or wrong answer. But do not be rash about selling your important dreams for a relationship.

My advice would be to wait for a girl who shares the same destination as you. You will connect so much better with someone who shares your dreams for the future. The more important things you give up for a girl, the higher the chance you will regret the decision later.

2. Different Speeds

When I went to school in Virginia, three or four times a year I would make the ten-hour drive back and forth to my home in New York. When I take long trips, my aim is not to make the trip comfortable or enjoyable but to reach my destination as soon as possible.

I stopped one time. During that stop I ate, got gas, and went to the bathroom. After that I just held it. I traveled over the speed limit (and I have the tickets to prove it). I did whatever it took to get home in the shortest amount of time. In the few times I carpooled the trip with some of my friends, I realized not everyone thought the same way about trips.

First, they announced they wanted to stop for *two* meals. OK… I can handle that. I was usually pretty hungry by the time I got home anyway.

Then I found out that not everyone can hold it as well as I can. We stopped for bathroom breaks every two hours. I found this quite annoying.

I thought to myself, "Why didn't you just go when we stopped for lunch an hour ago? And do you really need to buy another bottled water when we stop to go to the bathroom? Am I the only one that sees the link between drinking liquid and having to go to the bathroom?" But I just kept my thoughts to myself.

The kicker was when someone needed to stop and stretch his legs.

"Stretch your legs?! Is that so you can run home? Because that's what you are doing if you get out of this car."

People travel at different speeds, and the same is true in life. Some people like to have busy lives. They like to accomplish goals and realize achievements. They find tremendous pleasure in getting things done. They are readily able to make sacrifices for the sake of their purpose.

Others like to enjoy life. They stop and smell the roses. They get out of the car to stretch their legs. They find tremendous pleasure in their family and friendships and the play of life.

Few of us are fully at one of these extremes, but we each rest on a certain point along the spectrum. Maybe you're a relaxed guy, but your girlfriend is a superworker. She has all kinds of goals and ambitions in life, and she works like crazy to meet them. Somebody (and probably both of you) is going to have to compromise on your speed if you are going to ride in the same car.

Virtually everyone will have to compromise in this area to some extent because rarely will two people move at the exact same speed. But how much are you willing to compromise? It would be pretty difficult for an extreme "speed" person to live with an extreme "scenic-route" person and vice versa. You can do it, but it will take a lot of compromise. And only you can answer the question, "How much compromise am I willing to make?"

3. Different Routes

Sometimes your destination is the same, but you want to take different routes. At one point, one of my friends had his eye on a girl who was graduating high school. They both loved the Lord deeply and wanted to be missionaries. They got along great, and it seemed like she was showing a real interest in him, too. The only problem was that she was going to be a doctor, so she was going away to college and medical school. That threw at least an eight-year waiting period on any hope of a relationship. Something could still happen between these two, but it will not be until their divergent paths connect again in the future. For now they are taking different routes.

Routes can diverge for a number of reasons. A guy and a girl might take separate paths because of education, work, ministry, family responsibilities, and any number of other things. This is not normally a permanent block to a relationship, but rather a major delay.

Remember that with each of these categories, if a difference exists, you have a choice to make. You can give up the girl, or one of you will give up your travel plans. You can't have both. That choice is up to you, but soberly acknowledge what you are giving up. Don't make any reckless decisions. We are talking about the rest of your life.

BEWARE OF THE DUST BUNNIES

Many young women in the world long to be married. Much of their vision for the future is tied up in being a wife and a mother. And absolutely nothing is wrong with that. But some of them attempt to improve their chances of getting married by taking on no direction for their lives. They think if they have no personal direction, then they can conform to the direction and calling of whomever they fall in love with so they won't have any conflicts. Their purpose in life is a liquid that just fills whatever shape it finds itself in.

When I was growing up, my father called people like this "Dust Bunnies." I never completely understood what he meant until I lived in China. You can hardly find a house with carpet there. Every floor is either linoleum, tile, or wood. If you don't sweep regularly, all the dust from the apartment will gather on the floor and form dust bunnies. These look like little tumbleweeds made from dust. They just sit in dirty corners or underneath couches or beds.

They sit there until something comes near them. Then they follow anything that moves. Because they are so light, anything with a static charge draws them like a magnet. If somebody walks by, they will float after him. Then when another person comes back the other way, they will chase after him. They aimlessly follow anything that has direction because they have no purpose of their own.

Personal direction in life is part of what it means to be a complete person. For a girl to find part of her future in serving her husband's plans and calling is natural, but she must have a sense of personal purpose as well. If she does not get married right away, will she just float around like a dust bunny wasting her life away? Is that the kind of person you want attached to you for the rest of your life? A purposeless parasite that sucks her sense of purpose from you? I sure hope not.

You don't want a girl with no direction. You want a girl with the same direction. Do not confuse the two. Is she pursuing a future advancing God's kingdom, or is she waiting for a guy to tell her what to do with her life? You want to link lives with a girl who is running the same direction as you. If she is already running without you, then you know she will keep running with you. Do not pick up a girl who is seated at a crossroads waiting for anyone with a direction to give her a ride. If the road ever gets tough, she will be a burden because she is only coming that way to follow you.

Let me also say many people do not have a strong sense of direction in life while in high school and even college. This is normal. They are still going through the process of hearing from God and discovering what they excel at and enjoy doing in life. But if someone is out of school and still has no sense of direction for the future, then that can be a sign of aimlessness in life.

Your sense of direction is something that lives deep within your heart and is almost always God-given. It is a treasure. Do not trade it for a relationship. Wait for the Lord to unite your life with someone who shares the same purpose He has given you. How much more fulfilling that life would be.

So be diligent to check that any potential love interest lines up with the same direction you have in life. Do not get months into a relationship before you discover this incompatibility. It's a long trip, so make sure you have the right person in the car.

THE LIST TEST:
Is she what you have been looking for?

One day when I was 22 years old, I was thinking about three different girls that I thought were absolutely great. All of a sudden a question popped into my head, "If I could marry any of these three girls, who would I choose?" The first thought in my mind was, "Toby, you have no chance with any of these girls, let alone all three of them. Instead of imagining how to deal with impossible situations, let's work on something more useful, like calculus." But then I thought, "Wait, I should have some way to decide between girls who meet my basic standards, in case I ever do face such a situation. Marriage is too important to make such a decision without thinking about it first." So the rest of that afternoon I looked through the Bible, brainstormed, and reflected on what was important to me to make "The List."

The List is my typed out standards for what I want in a wife. It is, on paper, what I am looking for in a woman. It contains the standards I will not compromise and the deep longings of my heart for the woman I will share my life with. Such a list is important for several reasons.

WHY A LIST IS IMPORTANT

First, we need to have a firm grip on our standards for a marriage partner so we don't begin to compromise when we are in the throes of infatuation. A list of standards protects us from making a permanently bad decision based on temporarily good feelings.

If you do not have such a list, you lack the protection of objective standards. You are at the mercy of your intelligence and willpower in the state of infatuation. If you are like me, that is a bad place to be.

If your list is only in your mind, then you will have a much easier time rationalizing it away when under the intoxicating effects of attraction. So write it down; make it permanent. Protect yourself.

Second, if we have a list of objective standards, we are able to avoid the distraction of dead end relationships. We will know if someone is the right kind of person for us to date before we even start.

Mike Holloway was a pole vaulter who had endured two straight years of disappointing performances. After several solid performances in the early '90s, he had dropped way below the level of international competition. Then came the 1996 Olympic trials. In the previous months, Holloway had seen that he had the potential to vault much higher than he had ever before in competition. So he made a decision. He decided not to enter the competition until the necessary jump neared his previous career high. No warm-ups. No building his confidence. Just waiting.

He bent side-to-side to stretch his legs as the others were doing the lower jumps. Then when the bar was raised higher than he had ever cleared in competition, he got in line to jump. When his turn came, he grabbed his pole and set his feet. He took three deep breaths while he pictured a perfect jump in his mind. Then he exploded down the track, put his pole down perfectly, and jumped with all his might. He cleared the bar. As he landed on the padding, the crowd erupted into cheers. He had smashed his previous personal record and won the trials with a vault of 19'-¾". When asked by a frantic reporter why he didn't start jumping until the bar was raised past his personal best, he answered, "I didn't want to waste my strength at lower heights."

But many of us do just that in relationships. We waste our time, energy, and affections on women who are not the kind of person we are looking for in a wife.

In the movie *That Thing You Do,* Faye, the character played by Liv Tyler, laments after a painful breakup, "I have wasted thousands and thousands of kisses on you. Shame on me for kissing you with my eyes closed so tight." She realized that her infatuation had blinded her to the years she was wasting on a man not worth marrying.

Proverbs 31:3 says, "Do not spend your strength on women, your vigor on those that ruin kings." What a waste to spend our strength and energy in relationships that should never exist. If we just set some objective standards for ourselves, we would not squander our lives on women we would never marry.

Third, a written list helps us know exactly what to ask God for in our future wife. God loves to fulfill the desires of those who love Him. Just like a good father loves to lavish presents on his children, our Dad in heaven wants to bless us with every good thing we can ask for. If the things you are looking for in a wife will bless you and don't conflict with God's plan and purposes for your life, He would love to give them to you.

Fourth, the list can serve as a special confirmation when the time comes for us to move forward in a relationship. When my wife was a young girl, her family found themselves in a situation where they had to move an hour away with little money to begin renting a house. Each weekend they would go and look at houses in the area with no luck whatsoever. Everything was either junky, in a terrible neighborhood, or out of their price range. Her mother began to compile a list of things they were looking for to help them choose between their mediocre options. However, the list soon turned into the family's wish list for a dream house. Each family member added their hopes.

My wife's older brother wished for a basketball hoop and a paved driveway. She and her sister each wanted her own bedroom. Their mom wanted a covered porch, and their dad wanted an office. There were dozens of other wishes on the list too. And it needed to fit in their price range.

After another disappointing weekend finding nothing they were looking for, their family decided to check out one last house in a neighboring town. As they pulled up to the house, her brother gasped and said, "Look, guys. A basketball hoop. And a paved driveway." And her mother exclaimed, "And a covered porch." And that was not all. There was a yard to play in, a back deck, and a two-car garage.

Each family member was trying not to get too hopeful, but the excitement showed on each of their faces. The owner let them in, and they began to swarm throughout the house.

The kids shouted down from the second floor, "There are three bedrooms up here."

"And two downstairs." her dad answered.

"That's five bedrooms!" her mom screamed.

"That's one for each of us!" the girls squealed in unison.

"And an office for me." her dad exclaimed.

As they ran throughout the house, they found everything they had wished for: a basement laundry room, extra kitchen cupboards, a place for the dishwasher, sliding glass doors, a separate dining room, and a den. It was everything they had dreamed of and more.

But then her dad gently touched her mom's arm and whispered, "Honey, there is no way we can afford this house. This is twice as good as anything we have looked at."

But then the owners offered them a price that was half the going rate. And they told them they could bring their pets. Each member of the family began to weep with joy at the miracle unfolding before them.

God had blessed them by fulfilling every wish. And because they had written them down, they were able to see the greatness of His provision.

COMMON LIST PROBLEMS

Many people (in my experience, especially girls) have already written out such a list. Or at least they have a list somewhere in their minds that they consciously or subconsciously use to evaluate potential future partners. However, often one of three problems plagues their lists.

First, the list is so ridiculously demanding and specific that the person is forced to choose between never getting married or feeling guilty for compromising the List. The point of the List is not to find a perfect husband or wife. You will be searching forever because there aren't any. The point is to protect your high standards from the power of infatuation.

The second problem is that the List is so general or the standards are so low that it is useless. The list is powerless because the bar is set so low anyone can crawl over it. Maybe the list consists of things like "nice" or "a good person." Usually, the list makers are afraid that if they set the standards too high, they will never get married. So they set their standards so low they don't rule anybody out. This makes the list pointless. It is only useful if it is effective in ruling out people who should not be considered for marriage.

In the third problem, the person has a good list, but he is not committed to it so it loses its power. This person has done a great job of compiling the right kind of list. The only problem is he does not use it. A list is only as useful as the commitment to it. It can be a powerful tool to protect you from bad relationships before they start, but you must use it. If you do not consult it when you are considering starting a relationship, then it is just a piece of scrap paper.

HOW TO MAKE YOUR LIST

The first step in making your List is to list everything that you desire in a wife. No matter how ridiculous it seems to you, write it down. If you want her to be intelligent, write it down. If you'd like her to be 6 feet tall, put it down. If you want her to have a doctoral degree, list it. If you want her to be an astronaut, jot it down. If you wish she were raised by wolves deep in the Amazon forest, you know what to do.

Think about different categories of standards: Christian commitment, character, cultural background, personality traits, looks, family background, church background, hobbies, health, skills, attitudes, and values. For each category, write down all the qualities you would love to have in your wife.

I have provided a place for you to do this at the end of the chapter. Take a moment right now and do the exercise I just described. Use the categories I listed above to help your brainstorm.

Write down both things you want her to have and things you want her to *not* have. You should not only have qualities like "Christian" and "funny." Also, include all the qualities that you do not want her to have, such as "not quarrelsome" or "not lazy."

Often our first tendency in making such a list is to simply imagine a girl we like and start describing her. But you want a list that is objective and not influenced by your infatuations. Try to think of qualities, not of people. As you brainstorm, many girls will probably come to mind that embody a certain characteristic. That is okay. But do not allow one girl to control your list.

When you are finished brainstorming all the things you could ever wish for, read over the list. This is your dream girl. If you had to build a robot to marry, these would be your specifications. If you could have your way about every little thing, this is how she would turn out.

Second, go through your list and put a checkmark next to anything on which you will absolutely refuse to compromise. Record each quality you will not give in on, no matter what else lines up. You are the one who has to live with your wife, so be as picky as you want to be. This will normally consist of somewhere between 8 and 15 items. Any less is probably not having high standards in enough areas. And if you have many more than 15, you might be going overboard. Remember, this is not everything you want but only your absolute necessities.

Now take each of the qualities you just put a check next to and write them down at the end of this chapter under the heading "Must Have." Take time to do it right now.

This list is the bare necessities a person must have for you even to consider dating, courting, or marrying her. No matter how good looking she is or what other great qualities she has, if she does not fulfill every quality on this list, she is not an option. These are your non-negotiables. No compromise is possible here. This part of your list helps serve as the guide to keep you from wasting your strength on lower heights. Again, do not even consider a girl if she does not fulfill all these qualities. On the next page is the list I wrote down of my non-negotiable characteristics.

As you look at my list of "Must Haves," you might think I am superficial or that my standards are too high or too low. Each person's List will be different. Maybe you could care less about intelligence, but having a partner that is physically affectionate is a "Must Have" for you. Perhaps a good sense of humor is crucial to you, or you are unwilling to marry someone from a different stream of Christianity. Possibly you think I put too much emphasis on good looks or even too little. Your list will reflect you and your standards. You are free to prioritize whatever qualities are important to you, but you would do well to include those discussed in the Bible Test.

Third, go through your first "If I Could Design a Wife" list and put a line through any quality that is not important to you. These are things that you wrote down in your brainstorming, but they aren't truly significant to you. For example, maybe you wrote down that she have blue eyes. If that is just what you would choose if you were building a wife but it is not truly important to you, than cross it off.

This does not mean to cross off everything that did not go on the "Must Have" list. We have dreams for our wives that are not

> **Toby's MUST HAVE List:**
>
> ✓ Good Chance of Staying Thin
>
> ✓ Pretty Face
>
> ✓ Christian
>
> ✓ World-Changer Attitude
>
> ✓ Emotionally Healthy
>
> ✓ Smart Enough for Me to Share My Thoughts With
>
> ✓ Some Area of High Gifting (I would like her to really excel in an area, whether it is art, sports, public speaking, hospitality, etc.)
>
> ✓ Not Obsessively Materialistic
>
> ✓ Highly Moral
>
> ✓ Humble (willing to say sorry, willing to get accountability)
>
> ✓ Forgiving
>
> ✓ Relatively Selfless (she doesn't need to be Mother Theresa, but she must at least be characterized as a selfless rather than a selfish person)

absolute necessities. But they are things that are important to us. For my friend Taryn, having a husband that was a tennis player was important to her. You may think that is the least important thing in the world, but that is why you get to make your own list.

    Do not cross off things as unimportant because you think they should be unimportant. There are no right or wrong answers here.

These are any things that are important to you. It might be about her hobbies, her body, her faith, her sexual history, her talents, or her life dreams. Nothing is off limits. If it is important to you, don't cross it off.

After you have crossed out everything that is truly unimportant to you, take the remaining characteristics and write them under the heading "Want to Have." This is the second part of your final list. Look at mine as an example.

Toby's WANT TO HAVE List:

✓ Stunningly Beautiful Face

✓ Comes from Healthy Family

✓ Taller than Average (I am 6'5", so…)

✓ Athlete

✓ Very Smart

✓ 5 Talent Person (very gifted in many areas)

✓ Great Communicator

✓ Wise Decision Maker

The characteristics on this list are often totally new ideas from what you put on the "Must Have" list. For example, in my list I talk about having a healthy family in the second list, but don't even mention it in the first.

Other times this list will contain qualities that raise the bar from the base standard you set in the "Must Have" list. I take a "pretty face" and raise the standard to a "stunningly beautiful face" on the "Want to Have" list. Take some time to go back and look at your "Must Have" list. Is there anything you want to add to your "Want to Have" list that is raising the standard? If so, write it in.

Just because these standards are not "Must Haves" does not mean they are unimportant. It also does not mean that if a girl meets all your "Must Haves" that she is a good match for your list. If a girl did not meet at least a majority or maybe even three-quarters of my "Want to Have" list, then I would not consider her a good match. These sum up what you would like in your wife. Why would you marry someone who only met your absolutely lowest standards? Hold out for a girl who is the fulfillment of your longings and prayers.

However, if I met a girl who fulfilled all my hopes, except she was not athletic, I would still be open to her as a potential partner. You are willing to make some small compromises in these areas because you realize that no person is absolutely perfect. But be patient and watch God amaze you by giving you the girl of your dreams.

He did it for me. My wife, Micaela, is everything I asked for and even more. She literally fulfills every desire on my list, and she came with tons of bonuses, too. After I made my list, I knew the kind of woman I was waiting for; and when I met Micaela, I knew I had found her. God delights to give us the desires of our hearts. Don't be afraid to ask.

Now that you have created a list of what you want, why don't you take some time to specifically ask God for a person with the qualities you listed here. He loves to give His children good gifts.

Also, use the list to protect yourself. Do not allow yourself to stumble into a relationship with a girl who does not match your list. These are the desires God has put in your heart. Don't settle for anything less.

Brainstorm List:

Must Have:

Want to Have:

FUZZY MATH TEST:
Does being with her make me a better person?

I was slouched in the back seat of the car, pouting. My dad and his friend were driving me to a Christian winter camp in central New York. I was coming to the camp late, directly from my high school basketball game.

It had been the worst game of my life. I had not scored a point, and you couldn't count my turnovers using your fingers. Actually, it had been the culmination of a disappointing season. I was averaging less than five points a game. I had been a contributing starter the year before as a sophomore, and now I couldn't even score a point. I felt totally dejected.

My dad and his friend offered all the advice and consolations they could muster, but they could do nothing to make me feel better. I loved basketball, and I hated stinking at it. As we rode on in the silence, one voice echoed in my mind. It was the voice of my coach,

Mr. Ludeman. During a recent team meeting he had said, "One thing will destroy a basketball player's game faster than any other thing. No, it is not an injury. It is a girlfriend."

We would just laugh at him. We were the most popular guys in school. Girls liked us. And we liked them. How could a girl destroy our season?

But as I rode in the car that night, I had to wonder. I was in the midst of my first ever relationship and my basketball season was a wreck. Maybe, just maybe, Mr. Ludeman was right.

That weekend at the camp my girlfriend broke up with me. I was heartbroken. The end of my first love. A few days after I returned from camp, I went to my first basketball game since the breakup. I scored 15 points! And for the rest of the season I averaged 12 points a game. Maybe Mr. Ludeman knew what he was talking about after all.

Do I think that every relationship will destroy a basketball player's game? No. I don't. But I do think Mr. Ludeman understood something that many of us don't. Many relationships take more away from you than they give back. They distract you, and the rest of your life suffers because of it. But it does not have to be that way.

FUZZY MATH

Do you know what fuzzy math is? It is a new method of teaching math in some schools that focuses on what we think about math rather than on right and wrong answers. It wants to teach through understanding instead of rote and memorization. One of the phrases used to represent (and mock) this new style of teaching is $2 + 2 = 5$. To many Americans, it seems ridiculous to not be fact-focused when studying math. If you add two pieces of candy to two other pieces of candy, you are never going to get five. And if a first grader is expecting that, he will find himself sorely disappointed. It is a matter of fact, not subjectivity or opinion.

Marriage, however, operates on the fuzzy math principles. Marriage is not simple addition. It is math so complex we cannot reduce it to simple equations. We only know what the results are going to be through testing, or, for many people, trial and error.

Sometimes a guy and girl will get together and somehow they are so much better than they ever were apart. Everyone around them knows it. We say things like, "They are so good together." A wonderfully mysterious element exists that takes a good guy and a good girl and makes a fantastic couple. They are more fun when they are together. If they work together, maybe they are both more effective workers when they are on the same project. They are better people for being together. They are more successful, godly, happy, kind, and disciplined. These couples truly show that sometimes a relationship between a guy and a girl will look like $2 + 2 = 5$. They are greater together than they ever could have been separately.

This is how it is supposed to be. Ecclesiastes 4:9-12 says, "Two are better than one, because they have a good return for their work: If one falls down, his friend can help him up. But pity the man who falls and has no one to help him up! Also, if two lie down together, they will keep warm. But how can one keep warm alone? Though one may be overpowered, two can defend themselves." The author understood that there is tremendous power when two people add to each other's lives. As he observed the world, he saw that in the practical situations of keeping warm at night and winning a fight, two people are better than one. The same should be true in a marriage. Whether in doing ministry, starting a business, or raising a family; two should be better than one.

We have all seen sports teams that were greater than they should have been for each individual player on their team. The 2004 NBA finals are a great illustration. It was the Los Angeles Lakers vs. the Detroit Pistons. There have been All-Star teams that were inferior to the 2004 Lakers. They had Shaquille O'Neal, Kobe Bryant, Karl Malone, and Gary Payton in their starting lineup. Each of them was one of the greatest players ever at his position. The Detroit Pistons, on the other hand, were a ragtag bunch of players. You had Ben Wallace – a defensive center who could manage to shoot an air ball from 4 feet away. Rasheed Wallace – a hotheaded forward who had set NBA records for the most technicals. Tayshaun Prince and "Rip" Hamilton – possibly the two skinniest players to ever play in the NBA. And their MVP, Chauncey Billups, was a journeyman guard who had played for five teams in his first seven years. Not a team you'd expect to find in the NBA finals. But they worked hard, and they played together unselfishly.

All the matchups seemed clearly in favor of the Lakers, but the series turned out quite differently. The Pistons trounced the Lakers in five games. The best team beat the team of the best players. There was an intangible element on both teams. Something about the teamwork and interaction of the players on the Pistons caused them to play much better as a team than anyone would expect from their players. And the Lakers somehow managed to underachieve far below their potential.

In relationships, many situations turn out just like the Lakers. A guy and girl will start dating, and it becomes apparent to everyone that they were better off separate. The other areas of their lives are all effected negatively. Their devotional lives go downhill. Maybe they drag each other into the mire of sexual sin. Their grades begin to suffer. They are distracted at work. Their friends don't like to hang out with them when they are together. They are less fun, less holy, less focused, less disciplined, and less selfless. They are just less. This type of relationship could be represented by the equation 2 + 2 = 3. By some mysterious factor they are less powerful together than they are individually.

Please understand this: the Fuzzy Math Test is not measuring the quality of the girl you are considering. It is measuring her effect on you. She could be a godly, wonderful woman, but the two of you have a bad effect on each other.

When I reflect on the two girls I dated during my college years, I see the fuzzy math principle at work. Both girls were great Christians, highly moral, intelligent, and committed to serving God with their lives. I had a "2 + 2 = 5 relationship" with the first girl. She encouraged me spiritually. We did ministry together. She challenged my intellect. Our relationship was marked by absolute purity. Everyone loved to be around us when we were together. She truly made me a better person.

However, the other girl had the exact opposite effect. We never encouraged each other spiritually. In fact, it was the time where I was probably the farthest from God. My friends began to drift away. We wasted (not spent) tons of time together. We fought constantly. It was the ultimate example of a "2 + 2 = 3 relationship."

WHY DO WE AFFECT EACH OTHER THIS WAY?

If both girls were the same in so many key ways, then why were the relationships so markedly different? I cannot completely explain the fuzzy math effect, but I do know some of the factors that contribute to it.

1. Value Factor

The Value Factor simply looks at how much the two of you value each other. Your immediate reaction might be, "Of course we value each other. Why else would we be together?" But many times we slip into relationships where at least one of us does not truly value the other. We harbor secret thoughts that whisper, "I could do better than her." That thought is poison to any relationship. Unless you are utterly convinced that this girl is a prize you didn't deserve that God chose to bless you with, your relationship is in trouble. Seeds of dissatisfaction will bring a harvest of regret.

One time my friend said of a past relationship, "Deep down I just knew I could do better. I loved her, but I continually had this sense that she owed me something." This guy will always be dissatisfied and the girl will wear herself out trying to please him.

To have a "2 + 2 = 5 relationship," both people must value each other tremendously. It is this high sense of value that helps inspire us to be more than we were on our own. We want to be better spiritually because we respect the spiritual life of this wonderful girl. We try harder in school because we want to be the kind of person who should be with such a fantastic woman. We begin to lift ourselves to be the kind of partner this person deserves. Meanwhile, the girl thinks just as highly about you and is inspired to grow into the kind of person you deserve. This mutual inspiration takes both the man and the woman to a new level.

2. Origins Factor

I think that some significant differences exist between men and women. I bet you have noticed, too. One major area of differences is what they receive from a relationship. Both guys and girls come in many different personalities, so these differences are not hard and fast rules, but they are true in a large majority of cases. What a guy hopes to get out of a relationship is significance. In every area of life, a man wants to feel significant. To feel like he has accomplished worthwhile things. When he goes out with all his effort and wins the heart of a girl that was difficult to win, he feels significant. He is someone special because he won her heart. It could have been won by another man, but he was better, so he won it. Also, this will cause him to value her tremendously. She is his treasure; the one he sought.

A girl, on the other hand, hopes to have her need for security met in a relationship. If a girl is pursued by a man before she ever gives any evidence of falling for him, then she can feel secure in his love. She reasons, "He loved me before I ever did anything for him, so his love must not be based on my actions." And she is right. She can be free to respond in love because she feels secure that she does not have to earn his affections. This is a "2 + 2 = 5 relationship" in the works.

If the pursuer/responder roles are reversed, sometimes there can be a problem. When a relationship begins with the girl initiating and pursuing the guy, neither person gets what he or she longs for out of the relationship. The guy does not feel like he has won the heart of his beauty. He does not have a sense of significance or accomplishment. He knows that it was easy for him to have this girl's heart. That plants seeds in his mind of dissatisfaction. He thinks, "If this girl is what I get without trying, then I must be able to do better if I did try." And she is not highly prized in his eyes.

The girl can never feel secure because she suspects that her man only likes her because she liked him first. That means she must continually earn his affections. This can lead to her giving herself sexually to keep him interested in her. She cannot say, "No," because the foundation of the relationship is her giving to get his love. Most likely she will burn herself out trying to please him until she becomes completely dissatisfied as well. So this type of beginning often results in the man not valuing the girl and the girl destroying herself for the man. This is the foundation of a "2 + 2 = 5" relationship.

3. Habit Factor

Sometimes both people value each other tremendously, but their relationship still affects each of them negatively. Often these couples have simply allowed negative habits to be built in their relationship. Your habits of interaction will profoundly affect the influence you have on each other.

The girlfriend of one of my friends told him, "I don't like it when you are always trying to help me grow spiritually. Everyone else in my life tries to make me a better person. Let's just enjoy each other." And with that input they established a pattern of not talking about spiritual things together. Do you think this relationship was a positive one? Of course not. It went straight down hill.

Maybe a habit of wasting time is established. Your interactions consist mainly of watching TV or movies together. I think of a young couple I know whose TV watching has shot through the roof since they have been together. Or perhaps when you are together your time is just spent sitting around or wasting your time in other ways. Will you be a growing, successful couple? No way. You have established habits of apathetic time wasting. I am not saying there is no place for spending quiet, romantic time together. I love that time. But if the fruit of your relationship is not clearly seen in serving others and God, then is it a good relationship?

Habits of sexual sin also create destructive patterns in relationships. In high school two of my good friends were dating, and I watched as they began to be involved in a sinful way physically. Soon their entire relationship became polluted by that sinful habit of interaction. Their relationship was warped because the only fruit of their interaction was sin.

On the other hand, good habits can make your relationship an incredibly positive influence in your lives. If you pray and study the Bible together, you will see your spiritual life go to the next level. Couples that challenge each other spiritually and hold each other accountable experience incredible spiritual growth. Doing projects together, studying your interests together, and helping each other achieve goals will result in personal success like never before. It is important to make decisions to establish the right kind of habits at the beginning of your relationship to set the foundation for a positive future.

4. Emotional Health Factor

Another dynamic in the fuzzy math phenomenon is the individual emotional health of each person in the relationship. If one or both people have deep insecurities or other major emotional issues, the relationship will be short-circuited from having any positive effect. When I was a youth pastor, there was a young couple in my youth group who began dating. They were both great teens, but the young man was a young Christian and still had some major insecurities to work through. This caused him to be quite selfish and manipulative. His fears also caused him to be unmotivated. It soon became apparent that this young girl was being dragged down. No matter how much love and effort she poured into her boyfriend, he was not being pulled up to her level. She began to drift from her friends, underachieve in school, and develop negative attitudes. This lasted for over a year until the relationship finally ended in a painful breakup.

No matter how hard you try or what you do, the emotional problems of one person will pollute the relationship. Until both people are healthy individuals, it can never be a "$2 + 2 = 5$ relationship." How can a needy person be added to a relationship with the result of something positive? It can't happen. A needy person will always take. It takes a whole, healthy person to be able to give. And when two healthy people get together, we can see the wonderful phenomenon of $2 + 2 = 5$.

NO RELATIONSHIP IS NEUTRAL

Another important part of the fuzzy math effect is that there are no "$2 + 2 = 4$ relationships." Neutral relationships do not exist. Either you build each other up or you tear each other down. You are pushing each other closer to God or you are distracting each other from your First Love. Do not view your relationship as having no effect on you. Ruthlessly examine it to see what influence you have on each other. If you have been dragging each other down in only a few months, just think what could happen over a lifetime.

WHAT TYPE OF RELATIONSHIP DO I HAVE?

Most likely you immediately know what type of relationship you have. You instinctively know whether you are being built up or torn down; but if you are unsure, ask yourself the following questions about the different areas of your life.

Spiritual

✓ Am I closer or farther from Jesus because of this relationship?
✓ Do we pray for each other?
✓ Do we take time to study the Bible and pray together?
✓ Do we keep each other accountable in our devotional lives?
✓ Has our relationship led us into sexual or other types of sin?

Social

✓ Do my friends like hanging out with us when we are together?
✓ Am I drifting farther from my close friends because of this relationship?
✓ Am I more or less involved in church since we have been together?
✓ Do I hear people talk about how good we are together?

Success

- ✓ Have my grades slipped since this relationship started?
- ✓ Has it caused my performance at work to decline?
- ✓ Am I more or less disciplined now than before the relationship?
- ✓ Do our interactions lead toward accomplishing meaningful things or do they tend to waste time?

Sentiments

- ✓ Am I more happy or sad since I began this relationship?
- ✓ Do I find myself with less energy since we started dating?
- ✓ Do I frequently feel encouraged and challenged by my partner?
- ✓ Do I feel recharged or drained after I hang out with her?

After reading that list of questions, you probably feel one of two ways. You might be feeling great. Now you know that you have an awesome effect on each other. Or you might be feeling rotten. It is inescapable. You pull each other down. If you are the latter, you are asking, "Is this relationship doomed or is there hope to turn it around?"

I am going to be really honest with you. In my experience, it is tremendously difficult to turn a relationship like this around. I have been in a relationship like this, and I tried everything to fix it but to no avail. If you were married, then there would be no other option. With the grace of God and with lots of hard work this kind of relationship can be fixed, but it is definitely not easy. But now before you are married, reevaluating the relationship is probably best. I am confident you will find that your relationship fails many of the other tests in this book as well. It is most likely that this relationship will cause you myriad difficulties if you go on to get married.

BUILD UP OR TEAR DOWN

The summer after my junior year of high school I worked my first job doing construction on my church's new office building. The only reason I had this job was my dad was the pastor of the church, and they needed some cheap labor. I stink at doing anything with my hands, so construction was not my strong suit. Minimum wage was overpaying me for what I was able to contribute.

Now construction must be the longest, most boring job ever, but my friend Matt also worked on the site. This made the job a ton better, and we were able to enjoy the days working together.

When it came to construction, I looked up to Matt. His dad was a foreman and he had grown up doing construction jobs, so I assumed he knew what he was doing. One day, however, I learned otherwise.

We were putting up 2x4 beams in the roof of a building using a nail gun. Now a nail gun is a great tool. It allows certain stages of construction (like roofing) to go light years faster than what you could do with a hammer. It is incredibly helpful in construction. But it also has another side.

Because I was the amateur, I held the board in place while Matt nailed it in with the nail gun.

As Matt was firing the nail into the second board, I felt a sharp pain in my wrist.

He had shot me.

I dropped the board and looked down at my arm, but there was no blood. There was only a long red welt. The nail had hit me broadside. I was OK.

I took a couple deep breaths and told myself that this was a one-time phenomenon. I picked up the board and got back in place.

After successfully installing a couple beams, I was holding a board when all of a sudden I yelped in pain.

He had shot me again.

And luckily, the nail had hit me broadside again. I started thinking of all the horror stories of nails going through feet and hands and heads. You could really get hurt with these tools.

I don't know if it was wanting to appear brave or just plain foolishness, but I got back up there holding the board for Matt again.

The very next nail ricocheted off and cracked me right in the hand. I jumped off the ladder, looked at my third big welt, and shouted, "That's it. Now you hold the board."

Relationships are like a nail gun. They can build up or cause tremendous pain and destruction. They can be a tool of God or a weapon of the enemy. They are tremendously powerful. If that power can be channeled for good, you will see your relationship build you up in a way that nothing else can. But if that power is negative, it will tear your life down faster than you can imagine. That is why it is absolutely crucial to make sure your relationship passes the Fuzzy Math Test before you even consider moving forward.

ROMANCE TEST:
Am I really in love with her?

Before I met my wife, I would not have known to include this test. But that was before I fell in love with Micaela.

She is the most wonderful person I know. She is smart, caring, passionate, and fun. I have yet to lay eyes on a girl that holds a candle to her beauty. She still takes my breath away. And her purity, sense of destiny, and relationship with God set her apart from every other girl I have ever met.

I thought I knew what it was to be in love. Three years earlier, I had been in a relationship where I thought for sure we would get married. But when Micaela captured my heart, I experienced something that was light years beyond anything I had ever tasted before.

I am a pretty objective, even-keel guy, but I found myself overflowing with emotion. I would be sitting by myself thinking of her, and my whole body would tense up with the over-powering emotion I would feel.

I rarely bought gifts for past girlfriends, but the only thing I could think about when I was in any type of store was what I could buy for her. I would fall asleep at night thinking about what kind of flowers I could buy or how I could surprise her with them.

I don't think I had ever made a present for anyone in my life besides my mother. And that was only in preschool. After a few months with Micaela, I found myself buying supplies in craft stores. Next thing I knew I was building picture frames and clocks. With an overflowing heart, I wrote her love letter on love letter and poem after poem. She captivated me without even trying. I was totally smitten. I never knew anything was missing before, but for the first time in my life I knew what it was to be in love.

Now, if you have ever read a Christian book or heard a speaker about relationships, you know that what I experienced is called infatuation. Often you will hear two major points about infatuation. First, it will not last. Second, it is a horrible foundation for a relationship.

These are true. Although I do not plan to lose passion and romance from my marriage, I acknowledge that feelings will change and mature as our stages of life shift. If a relationship is built on the feelings of infatuation, when those feelings change the relationship is violently shaken. Infatuation cannot be the foundation.

But that does not at all mean that infatuation is unimportant or negative. God created it. It is terrific. It is the thing that makes poets write and singers sing. It is perhaps the most powerful, wonderful emotion that God instilled in humans. Infatuation is not meant to serve as the foundation but as the frosting. It is what makes love taste so grand.

Marriage must be built on a foundation of friendship and lifelong commitment. But you can't live in just a foundation.

Marriage must be more than that. If you just want a friend, then stay as friends. If you want a lover, there must be something more.

When I finished graduate school, I served as a missionary in Asia for a year. During my time there I began to study the Chinese language so I could communicate better. I soon learned that the Chinese system for writing is a whole lot different than English. In English (and most other languages in the world), we have an alphabet of letters that make up all the words we write. Chinese does not. Instead, every word in the language is represented by its own unique character (or picture) or a combination of two or three characters. This made it difficult for me to learn, but I grew to love it because many of the characters gave insight into the way the Chinese viewed that word.

The character for love is one of the most powerful examples. The top half of the character is the picture for "breathing into," and the bottom half of the character is the Chinese symbol that represents friendship. Thus, love is when friendship is breathed into. I love that. Infatuation is the mysterious breath that comes down on normal friendship and brings it alive into romantic love.

Now most of us in life chase after the breath. We make foolish decisions in relationships because we overemphasize infatuation, chemistry, and attraction. That is why I wrote this book: to provide tests to protect us from making a devastating choice while we are drunk on love.

But this test is to make sure that you do not reduce love to an objective choice. A quality person and a good friendship are not the only ingredients in a marriage partner. Love is so much more than that. Love has been enlivened by a heavenly breath. Friendship is the kindling that allows love to burn. But it must still be ignited with romance and passion.

If I had to choose between character and romance for a marriage partner, I would choose character. Romance can be readily ignited, but character rarely changes. But the good news is you don't have to choose. Don't settle for anything less than both.

HOW DO I KNOW IF I AM IN LOVE?

How do you know if you are in love? This is an important question. Like I said earlier, I had no idea I was missing anything until I fell for Micaela. The following are a few simple things you can look for that will tell you if you are truly in love with this person.

1. **Joy** – Do you enjoy being with her? Does she make you happy?
2. **Giving** – Do you find yourself naturally caring for her needs before your own?
3. **Desire** – Do you find the idea of sex with her to be thrilling?
4. **Longing** – Do you find yourself missing her when you are apart for any significant length of time?
5. **Awe** – Does your love fill you with a natural respect for her?

CAN I MAKE MYSELF FALL IN LOVE?

Is there any way to manufacture that special breath for a friendship? Perhaps you have a female friend who is awesome. You know she would pass any test you could throw at her. You've thought about something more, but the problem is you just don't have those feelings for her. Can that be fixed? Can you create those feelings?

I don't think you can create them. Romantic love is something that is there or isn't there. However, often times those feelings slumber within and can be awakened if given a chance. For example, I had known Micaela since I was 14 years old. And she was only 10. But one summer when I was in graduate school, she and her sister moved across the hall in my apartment building. By the end of that summer, I found myself falling in love with her. For the eight previous years I had known her, I would have told you that she was a friend and a great person, but love had not yet awakened in my heart.

The year before I met Micaela, I had a completely different experience. I was getting to be great friends with a female classmate. She was beautiful. She had a great mind. We connected like I do with few other people. We shared similar perspectives in life and hopes for the future. We just clicked really well as friends.

Of course, pretty soon both of us were wondering if we were supposed to be something more. We thought so highly of each other that we began to slowly walk in that direction. But we soon realized it wasn't working. We were just meant to be friends. No matter how great it seemed on paper, we did not have that extra breath.

Sometimes love will awaken in a friendship and sometimes it will not. The best we can do is give it a chance. Spend time together in groups. Allow your feelings to go toward the other person in that way. If a flame ignites, great. If not, then you still have a great friend, and God will bring someone else just as wonderful down your path.

UNREQUITED LOVE

I feel I should address what happens if your heart has fallen for someone, but she does not love you back. She is the girl of your dreams; she aced every test. Heaven is breathing all over the friendship from your perspective. But she just views you as a friend.

Well, I didn't tell you this before, but that is exactly the situation I found myself in with Micaela. I had fallen hopelessly in love with her, but she had never even thought of me in that way. She was even interested in another guy. But over the period of eight months I pursued her with everything I had, and now she is just as crazy about me as I am about her.

I want to share with you five practical steps to winning a girl's heart. This is not a list of romantic things to do to impress her. That will come in handy too, but you can find other books about that. This is a method for gently turning a friendship into something more.

1. Preparation

The first thing you need to do is make sure this is the girl for you to be pursuing. You do not want to begin convincing her to unlock her heart for you and then back out on her. Use the tests in this book to evaluate if she is worth the effort and risk you will need to put out to pursue her. This might not be easy, so you want to make sure you are working for a worthy goal before you start.

When I first fell for Micaela, I went through this preparation phase. I prayed about it, talked to my friends, consulted with my parents, pulled out my List, and examined her character next to the Bible's wise advice. No matter what test I threw at her, she passed with flying colors. She was awesome. But she was not yet feeling the same things in her heart for me.

2. Purposing

After the preparation, there comes a point where you need to make a decision. You must purpose your heart and say, "I am willing to patiently pursue this girl." I am not talking about giving it a shot for a week and giving up. Don't even bother trying. You want to win the heart of a great young woman. This will take time and work. Count the cost before you begin.

I was home on a Thanksgiving break from graduate school when I made the decision for Micaela. I committed myself for serious pursuit. I was not promising years of my life, but I consciously decided to work at winning her for at least the next eight months. That meant no other girls during that time and no giving up no matter how difficult it seemed during those months.

It might be wise to make a certain time commitment to yourself like I did. I think 4–8 months is a good time frame. It is long enough to give it your best shot, but not so long that you unnecessarily limit yourself. However you do it, the important thing is that you purpose in your heart to make a significant commitment to win her heart.

3. Permission

This is one of the most important and most misunderstood phases of convincing a girl you are the one for her. Most likely, this phase will be one significant conversation you have with the lucky lady. Two primary objectives must be accomplished in this conversation. If you leave out either one, you are hamstringing yourself in the pursuit.

The first is to let her know that you think she is so fantastic she is worth your significant time and effort to try to win her heart. Tell her why you think she is so great. Honestly praise the wonderful things you see in her. Let her know that if it is okay with her, you want to intentionally spend more time with her to get to know her better.

The second is to help assuage all the immediate fears that are going to rise up inside of her. She will most likely have several major fears. First, she will fear losing the friendship if she doesn't like you that way. Second, she will fear leading you on and hurting you. Third, she fears that you will act weird and make her uncomfortable.

You need to nip these fears in the bud during this first conversation. Let her know that being her friend is the most important thing to you. Even if nothing comes of all this, you will still be her friend. Let her know that she is not leading you on to spend time with you. You want to spend your time and effort pursuing her with the full realization that it might not work out. But you think she is so great that you want to anyway. Reassure her that you will not act weird. You are the same friend, but because she is so special you'd like to get to know her better.

Then give her time to think about it. She should not have to make a decision the night you spring all this on her. Give her time to think and pray about it. If she is as awesome as you think and you are both good friends, she will most likely give the idea a chance. But remember, you are asking permission. If she does say no, you must respect that. Perhaps you will have another chance down the road, but now is not the time.

When I was home from school during Christmas, I had "The Conversation" with Micaela. It was actually two conversations. In the first, I told her how special she was to me, and I asked her if I could begin to call her regularly. She did not have feelings for me, but she agreed anyway because she trusted me. She definitely still had her fears, but she was willing to give it a chance.

The night before I returned to college we had another talk where I gave her a chance to share her fears and concerns. Then I gave her a poem I wrote telling her how awesome she was. I was walking a fine line between scaring her away and showing her how special she was, but now it is something we both look back on with special memories.

One extra note. Depending on her family situation, it can be a good idea to ask her father for permission before you ever even ask the daughter. I know, I know. That ranks on the terrifying scale between having someone hold you under water and realizing you forgot your parachute mid-skydive. But it is important. It gives you credibility both with her and her family. And if her family likes you, it could gain you some extra support in the chase.

4. Pursuit

Here is where it begins to happen. You are beginning to woo the heart of your woman. This will be different for each person because you need to be yourself if you are going to convince her to like you. But a few general principles exist to help you.

First, you want her to spend time with you. If you share common friends, do things together with your group. If not, invite her to hang out with your friends. If she is open to the idea, go out on non-threatening dates like lunch or out for coffee. Now that the idea of romance between you is planted in her mind, you just need to give it a chance to grow. And that takes time together.

Second, keep a gentle tone of romance in the relationship. At first, this will probably be quite private. Maybe you occasionally send flowers. Or you could write her a poem. Or you could give her a gift. The possibilities are infinite, but the point is to show her she is special in your eyes. She is not just another friend.

Third, be sensitive to her reactions to things. For example, it might not be good to buy her a dozen long-stem red roses right away. That might be too much and make her uncomfortable. But few girls would feel weird if someone gave them yellow roses, carnations, or a nice bouquet. On Valentine's Day, I knew that Kay was still nervous so I bought her a single red rose with the note, "I am still hoping."

It might be a great idea to write her poems about how wonderful she is, but she might not be so keen on you reading them to her in front of all her friends. It is a delicate balance you must walk. On one hand, you must inject romance into a relationship where it is not yet natural; but on the other hand you can't move too quickly or too strongly, or you will make her uncomfortable. That is why the fourth principle is so important.

Fourth, be consistent. You must be a constant voice in her life telling her how special she is. I wouldn't try to overwhelm her with some extravagant demonstration of your love every few months. I would regularly (every week or two) do small, romantic things that make her feel like the most loved girl in the world. A time will come for the big things later, but you first need her to open her heart up to you.

When I was chasing Micaela, I actually lived 10 hours away at school. Soon after the Thanksgiving break I returned home for Christmas and was able to spend time with Micaela. I went over to her house often. (I am good friends with her siblings, too. How convenient.) We went out for coffee once. We hung out in groups a few times. And by the end of the break…

Nothing. Absolutely nothing. Actually, I think she was more scared than anything. But I returned to school and made it a practice to call her regularly–once or twice a week. We began to develop a strong friendship over the next few months from those phone calls. Very, very slowly the possibility of something more was opening up, but she definitely was not experiencing full-fledged romantic feelings for me yet. Throughout this time I would write her poems occasionally or give her a small gift of flowers. I would sometimes tell her on the phone how special I thought she was.

About five months into the pursuit it became obvious that she was beginning to share my feelings. I stepped up the pursuit. There were more flowers and big dates when I'd come home. But she was still tentative for another three months. Then she finally gave in and fell hopelessly in love with me too. It was a long, difficult process for me, but she was worth every minute of it. It was the best choice I ever made. I'd do it again in a second.

5. Perseverance

Here is the truth: It might not be quick. It might not be easy. With Micaela it was not until 7 or 8 months later that she was convinced enough to begin an official relationship with me. I went through moments of exhilarating triumph and seasons of deflating failure. So many times I wanted to give up. It hurt to keep trying and keep being rejected. But in those dark times I remembered that she was worth it and I kept going. And like a turtle's marathon, I slowly began to see progress. It was toilsome for over half a year, but now I have the girl of my dreams until death do us part.

But what if I had gone through that torturous half year and nothing worked out? I accepted that possibility at the beginning and decided that she was worth that risk. That purposed decision is what you need to persevere.

I can't promise you success. But I can promise you that this kind of pursuit builds the foundation for a great relationship. Like I said in Chapter 8, women long to be pursued. It will give her the security found in knowing that you first loved her. She does not have to earn your love. And for the rest of your life you will know that you won your highly valued treasure. You reached over your head and captured the heart of someone truly great.

HOW TO USE THIS BOOK

The first six months after I finished business school, I worked in my first management position. My friend from college owned an ice cream truck company, and I was his assistant manager for the season. One day my boss, Mike, asked me to install some padlocks on the chest freezers to protect us against theft. Ice cream is one hot commodity. He bought the brackets, the locks, the screws and handed me the drill to install them. He even did one for me so I could see what to do.

I need to interrupt the story at this point to remind you that I am completely incompetent when it comes to doing anything with tools, or my hands for that matter. So I sat there with a bag full of brackets, a case full of drill bits, and no clue how to do this correctly. But I didn't want to look stupid, so I just went for it. The first one took me a while to figure out, but pretty soon I was moving like a professional.

One screw, two screw, three screw, four screw. Next. One screw, two screw, three screw, four screw. Next. I was on a roll.

A couple hours later I was looking at the last freezer. I was so proud of myself. I was presented with a difficult challenge, and I had conquered. I began to install the last bracket.

One screw, two screw, three... I was having a lot of difficulty getting in the third screw. No matter how much strength I used, it wouldn't go in. But I would not be defeated. I propped myself up against another freezer, and using my legs for extra strength, pushed with all my might.

BAM! Something exploded inside the freezer. Then it began to hiss. I had hit some kind of gas line. The walls of the freezer began to bubble outwards. It was gonna blow. I ran around the corner and found my boss.

"Mike, Mike," I cried, "Come quick. I think I did something bad." Mike ran back around the corner with me. The freezer had stopped expanding, but each wall had blown out about 6 inches.

"What happened?!" Mike exclaimed.

I defensively said, "I was just screwing in the brackets like you showed me and all of a sudden, 'BAM! Hiss...' I didn't know what to do." Then Mike began to walk through to inspect my other work. At first he seemed impressed that I had done the whole job so quickly. Then he put his hand over his face and let out a long frustrated sigh.

He shook his head and whispered just loud enough that I could hear, "Toby, you screwed all the brackets on backwards." I looked; he was right. I had screwed each bracket on in a way so that when it was locked you could just unscrew the bracket and bypass the padlock. All that work was worthless. And in doing it wrong I placed the screws right near the freon lines, so I managed to destroy a $400 freezer in the process.

You see, a protection is powerless unless it is used correctly. It can even be destructive. The same is true of the tests in this book. They are a powerful protection against making a wrong choice in a marriage partner. But if you use them incorrectly, they will be ineffective at best. They may even cause confusion and hurt. So I have included this last chapter to help you understand the way I meant for this book to be used.

This book is not a score sheet. You should not take your girlfriend through these nine tests and give her a score. Actually, I have a confession to make. The first thing I did when I came up with the idea was to have one of my friends use it as a score sheet for a girl he was interested in. I know that is the temptation. As men, that is the way we think. Each one of us has, at some point in our life, sat in a room with other guys and ranked girls. Be a man. Admit it. Maybe it was a purely superficial "1 to 10 – Hot or Not" scale, or perhaps it was a less shallow "Looks Plus Personality" scale. Possibly you are too kind to assign a number value to a person, so you just created a ranking of every girl in your class or church.

I can remember one day during college when I was sitting in my dorm with my two best friends rating girls. We were concocting a ranking system that would put the college football BCS system to shame. We incorporated spirituality, body type, personality, chance of staying thin, integrity, and sense of humor. We even had different weights on each category to maximize our accuracy. Then we set the entire system on a minus ten to plus ten matrix to ensure differentiation. Now, is this a horribly degrading, slightly sub-human thing to do? Yes. But almost every guy has done it. Listen to me. Please don't use my book that way.

You may say to yourself, "If my girlfriend scores over an 8.3, within a month I'll be down on one knee." That is the wrong way to use this book. Why? Think about it. If Betty gets a seven out of nine, then I am thinking she lines up pretty good, right? Well, what if the two she missed were she is not a Christian and you are not romantically attracted to her. Then she is a horrible choice for a wife.

Instead of a scoresheet, this book should be used more like a college application. I remember being 17 years old and spending hours and hours filling out college applications. I had to write essays, tell them about my family's finances, give them my SAT scores, forward transcripts from my high school, and meticulously list every extracurricular activity. By the end, I had memorized my Social Security number and had a 500-word answer for what I wanted to do with my life. Then my mom helped me gather up all the sheets of paper, put them in order, and mail them off to the college. Then I waited.

Somewhere inside a conference room on a highly selective college campus, an admissions committee was trying to decide if they would let Toby Cavanaugh into their university. They weighed my test scores, my grades, my family's finances, my recommendations, my sports ability, my awards, and even my membership in the chess club to decide whether or not they would choose me. They were using a battery of individual tests to make a judgement about me. There were some things on which they would not compromise. If I flunked out of high school, they were not going to accept me, no matter what other redeeming qualities I possessed. If my references reflected a low opinion of me, then my chances of getting into the school were miniscule, as well. However, some unimpressive areas were acceptable if I made up for it in other important areas. They could look past me being a rather uninvolved high school student if I got a perfect score on my SATs, and they could overlook mediocre grades if I am one of the top 100 basketball recruits in the country. They are evaluating the whole of who I am using these individual tests.

This book should be used in a similar way. I believe that for some issues compromise is not an option. I will not marry an unbeliever. I will not marry without the approval of my key leaders. I will not proceed in a relationship if God clearly tells me, "No." However, in some situations a stronger area can make up for a weaker area. If we have some significant differences in personality, but the call of God on our lives lines up perfectly, then I can accept that. Or if one of your friends has some reservations about her but everything else lines up perfectly, then maybe you will choose her even though he objects. Just remember: a college has thousands of students every year, and they can expel anyone they regret accepting. But you only have one chance for marriage, and if it goes badly you will regret it for the rest of your life. Keep your standards high.

Second, do not use this book as a divining rod for locating a wife. A divining rod was a forked stick that was thought to have the magical ability to find underground supplies of water. The diviner would hold one fork of the stick in each hand and point the stem forward. Then he would wander aimlessly over the land until the rod would mysteriously dip down to where a well could be dug to find water. Do not use this book as some sort of magical talisman to help you find your soulmate wherever she has been buried. Proverbs 19:14 says, "Houses and wealth are inherited from parents, but a prudent wife is from the LORD." Let the Lord lead you to potential partners, then use this book as a test to see if they might be from Him. I am not saying that you must be dating a girl before this book will be useful, but it should be someone you have already been thinking about. Only use this book if you are already considering a girl. Don't use this book to try to jumpstart love for a random person.

Third, this book will not be helpful in actually acquiring an excellent wife. You see, finding a woman who passes all the tests is not the hardest thing. You will usually take notice when you meet a woman like that. The difficult thing is to convince her that she should be married to someone like you. To make a great catch, you need great bait. Focus on growing into a young man of excellence before you waste your time looking for a girl with whom you don't have a chance.

Finally, I cannot promise a perfect, or even an easy, marriage if you follow my advice. I am confident that using the tests in this book will greatly raise your probability of choosing a great wife and having an enjoyable life. But I am not willing to put a guarantee behind it. Marriage can be a risky proposition.

By using the wisdom contained in these tests, you will protect yourself from much of the danger inherent in making a lifelong commitment. But choosing a marriage partner is a little like eating food and drinking water in a third-world country. Eating food in a third world country can be dangerous. Many bacteria are in the food and water that will cause minor sicknesses in Americans. It is also possible to contract a serious illness, such as Hepatitis A or typhoid fever. I lived in Asia as a missionary the year that I wrote this book, and I learned that you should take many safety measures: never drink tap water, only eat fruit you peel yourself, avoid all shellfish, and make sure all meat is served hot.

Obeying these precautions will go a long way to protect you from sickness. But nothing can keep you absolutely safe in third-world conditions. Take it from a guy who has spent whole nights talking to the toilet bowl after getting food poisoning. Marriage is a risk. I happen to think that the greatness of marriage is more than worth that risk. Marriage can be the greatest earthly source of strength and joy you ever know. It can also be the most draining, discouraging, depressing, and demoralizing force in your life. If you are wise, you will do everything you can to eliminate as much of that danger as possible.

I also won't guarantee my advice for another reason. It is vital that each person take full responsibility for this choice. You cannot marry someone because your pastor told you so, because your parents told you so, because your friends told you so, or even because you think God told you so. Five years after the big day, when you are sleeping on the couch and brimming with anger over that huge fight, you need to be completely certain that you made the choice and gave your word that you would never leave her. No one else can be responsible for a promise of that magnitude. When you marry someone you must be fully conscious that this is your, and only your, choice. No one else is forcing you into it.

When I was 15, my grandma took my whole family to Florida. We went to Disney World, Universal Studios, and many other attractions. It was the vacation of a lifetime. One day as we were driving through Kissimmee, I was staring out the window at all the unique buildings. Then my eye caught something that made my jaw drop. It towered above the city skyline. It looked like it touched the clouds. I had seen one before, but only a fraction of this size. This one must have been over 30 stories high.

It was the world's tallest Skycoaster. If you don't know, a Skycoaster is somewhere in between a bungee jump and a giant swing. I tried to speak to get my family's attention, but all I could manage was to point and stutter. The eyes of my family members looked in the direction of my outstretched arm until each of them was staring slack-jawed, too. Like a moth subconsciously drawn toward the danger of a flame, my dad shifted course so we could see this terrible tower up close. The closer we got, the more and more difficult it became to keep my wide eyes focused on its peak. As our minivan finally pulled up to the base, I could no longer see the top, even by twisting my neck and pressing my face up against the window.

After we parked, I stepped out of the van and looked straight up. All I could mutter was an awed, "Whoa." After the whole family unloaded, we began to slowly walk toward the ticket office in silence, with all six of our faces pointed up.

Hanging on the window of the shop was a large black sign with all-capital white letters that described this colossus. We read, "Visitors will be placed in special flight suits and fastened to steel cables. Then you will start the agonizing one-minute ride to the top of the tower. Once you reach the height of 300 feet, you will hear our crew tell you, 'Three, Two, One. FLY!' Then you pull your own ripcord starting your plunge downward toward mother earth. You will free fall for 120 feet straight down, until the cables gently catch you and you start your swing out over the water reaching speeds of 85 mph."

Then we turned to face the monster and with open mouths watched as some brave adventurer was screaming at the top of his lungs as he was hurtling toward the earth faster than we had ever driven in a car. It was horrifyingly awesome. Something rose up deep inside me that wanted to conquer this thrill-park Babel. My mom and I turned to look at each other. I felt that courage fill my heart that you can only find when you are daring something great with someone close to you by your side. We both knew what we must do. As if sharing a mind, we said in unison, "Let's do it!"

We talked my little sister into joining us, and several $20 bills and waiver forms later we were off the ground in our three-person harness. Then our trying-not-to-tremble trio was climbing.

The next minute was about the longest of my life. It was longer than the tortured minute before my dad would come in to spank me; it was longer than the painful minute after I peed my pants in the middle of a 4th grade class; it was even longer than that cursed minute after I called my girlfriend by another girl's name during a farewell. When we finally got to the peak, I could see my ant-sized dad pumping his fist in encouragement.

Then a garbled voice blurted violently over a loud speaker, "Three." I closed my eyes.

"Two." I gasped one last breath.

"One." I braced myself.

"And FLY!" Nothing.

After a few seconds of nothing, I slowly unscrunched one of my eyes and looked at my mom. She looked over at me and my sister and said, "Are you sure you want to do this?" Then I remembered. The ripcord. No one else could make us fall. We had to pull the ripcord.

My sister and I looked at each other. We could see the fear in each other's eyes. We looked down. We could see my dad, brother, and Grandma cheering us on below. And then we locked eyes again. We both nodded and knew exactly what the other meant. Like one person we replied, "Yeah. Let's do it!" Then I reached back and found the ripcord.

And I pulled.

And I experienced the most exciting, terrifying, awesome ride of my life.

The fact is: ***nobody else can make you get married***. Sure, garbled voices will be shouting what you should do. Family and friends will be cheering you on from the ground. But only you can pull the ripcord.

You will never be able to blame this decision on the tests from a book. You can't pin it on what your pastor told you in his office. Your parents won't swear the vows of lifelong allegiance. And your friends can't say, "I do." Only you can pull the ripcord.

You bear the full responsibility for your choice. And remember, choose your partner well. If you do, you will experience a ride greater than you ever dreamed.

Acknowledgements

To Joanna, thank you for helping me get this book on the road to being published.

To Mary, thank you for cleaning up my writing while helping me keep my voice.

To Bethany, thank you for excellent work beyond what I could afford.

To Dad, thank you for encouraging me to step out and publish this book.

To Mom, thank you so much for all the painstaking work you did to make this possible.

To Micaela, thank you for being you. You are beyond what I deserve.

To Jesus, thank you for rescuing me out of darkness into your marvelous light.

About the Author

Toby Cavanaugh is the Director of Campus Target, a missions organization that brings young adults to Asia to ignite church planting movements on college campuses. He is a graduate of Elim Bible Institute and earned his MA in Practical Theology and MBA from Regent University. He is also an adjunct professor at Elim Bible Institute. An engaging speaker, Toby travels internationally with a message that God is inviting young adults to step out from the "normal" into the adventure for which they were born. Toby's home alternates between Asia and Lima, NY, with his wife, Micaela, and their young daughter, Maia.

For more information about Campus Target, check out www.campustarget.org.

To invite Toby to speak to your conference, church, or college ministry, you may contact him at toby@campustarget.org.

www.ingramcontent.com/pod-product-compliance
Lightning Source LLC
LaVergne TN
LVHW051838080426
835512LV00018B/2943